T0354397

CAGED
AND
LOCKED

My Personal Experience with
Circumstantial Depression

LẸWA UBUNIFU

Order this book online at www.trafford.com
or email orders@trafford.com

Most Trafford titles are also available at major online book retailers.

Print information available on the last page.

ISBN: 978-1-4907-9291-0 (sc)
ISBN: 978-1-4907-9290-3 (hc)
ISBN: 978-1-4907-9292-7 (e)

Library of Congress Control Number: 2018968562

Trafford rev. 12/29/2018

North America & international
toll-free: 1 888 232 4444 (USA & Canada)
fax: 812 355 4082

Contents

All my life,
I have wanted to belong.
All my life,
I have wanted to be loved,
Without judgement,
Without being bullied.
My heart is full,
Of the LOVE I have to give,
Of the love my Daddy gives me.
Every day, every hour, every minute,
Jesus has blessed me with a love,
So profound, so nourishing.
I love him, I love my Daddy,
More than life itself,
But he commands me to love people,
Despite of what my physical eyes see.
The greatest gift I can give,
My friends, my family, my associates,
my fans, you…
The greatest gift that I continually,
Chose to give you,
Is my time, my love, my heart!

I give this heart to you,
As a token of my appreciation.
My love, my friendship, and
For being a part of my life.
I hope that someday,
When I am long gone,
The time, love, creativity, and
Spirit of Lęwa Ubunifu,
Is what you remember,
Most About Me.
As we head into each new year,
I pray that this heart blesses you,
As much as it has blessed me,
Giving it to such a wonderful and
blessed person,
Like the one reading this book.
May you always feel the love,
That I have for you,
Through this amazing and
Blessed heart that I have made,
Especially for you!

I Am A Creative…

Don't try to put me in a box because I won't fit. Don't try and assign me a specific color because tomorrow I might be a different color. Don't try and put me in a specific group, for I am many groups. Don't try to label me with just one word, for there is not just one word for me. Don't try and look at me with one eye closed, for you might miss something important. Don't try and speculate what I feel, for my feelings are as vast as the sea. Don't try and psychoanalyze me, for I am always changing. Don't try and tell me what to wear, for I will always redesign the style. Don't try and assign me one job, for you will soon find me doing multiple jobs. Don't try and assume you know me because I guarantee you that tomorrow, you won't even recognize me.

I am a creative. I am every color in a Crayola Ultimate Crayon Bucket times infinity. I am every fish in the sea. I am every flower and tree in the world. I am every type of candy at Halloween. I am every time of ice cream you will ever eat. I am different from everyone you will ever meet. I am unique. I am a nerd, a loner, a prep, a thespian, a drifter, and an emo. I can be empathetic as well as callous. I can be happy and sad.

I am a creative who just wants to be accepted the way I am. Don't put restrictions on me or tell me what I can and can't do. I will just strive even harder to reach for the stars because…

I Am A Creative!!!

<u>WARNING</u>
Reflections in this book
may be distorted
by socially and
politically constructed
ideas of 'beauty',
'love', 'relationships',
'family', and 'self'

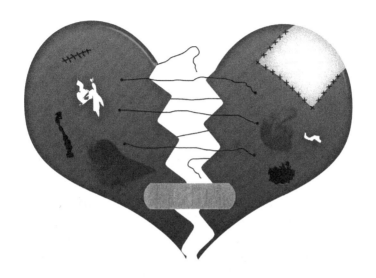

What Is Circumstantial Depression

Circumstantial or Situational depression, or Adjustment Disorder With Depressed Mood is a short-term, stress-related type of depression. It can develop after a person experiences a traumatic event, series of events, or a change in a person's life. Situational depression stems from a person's struggle to come to terms with the changes that have occurred. It can be very difficult for a person to cope or adjust to their everyday life following such an event or change. It's also known as reactive depression. Situational depression often goes away in time, and talking about the problem can ease the recovery process. Once the person is able to cope with the new situation, recovery is possible. In 2013, the mental health diagnostic system technically changed the name of "adjustment disorder" to "stress response syndrome."

How Is Circumstantial Depression Different Than Other Types Of Depressions

Depression is going to usually look different for everyone. There isn't a one-size-fits-all solution to depression because not all depression is the same. There are many types of depression. It is important to speak with a doctor you trust to treat and diagnose the type of depression that you have. A wrong diagnosis and wrong treatment of the incorrect depression type can have damaging effects and can leave you feeling worse and can lead to more severe symptoms and outcomes of your particular depression. Even though depression can be diagnosed correctly, symptoms can still vary from person to person and so can the depression itself. It is important that you let your voice be heard. One thing is for certain, depression is more than just feeling sad from time to time.

I can only speak from my personal point-of-view, but having been drugged up for over five years, being in counseling for over 15 years, and no one really listening to what I was really saying, I know what happens when certain types of depression go ignored. The various medications that I was on did nothing for me but make me fat and the counseling just made my depression worse. Depression also has a "happy memory lapse" effect. That means that happy memories in the brain tend to fade away, be forgotten, or slip out of the mind quickly. The depressed mind tends to remember harsh feeling memories over the good ones. They may not remember even the last time that they smiled or laughed or even had fun. While writing the "happy" memories down can help, it may take more than that to remember both the good and the bad. Taking a picture, recording a video, or other ideas such as these can trigger the good and happy memories, but sometimes, the memories are just tucked away and lost for good.

Forgetting the "happy" memories can also be the brain's way of protecting itself. If you can't remember anything "happy" or "good", then you put up a wall and protect yourself from everyone else in order to ward off anymore of the "bad" memories that you have felt in the past. You refuse to be hurt ever again and make sure that you try not to let anyone get too close to you. When people refuse to even try to get close to you, you shrug it off as if you don't care. Again it is important to talk to someone that you trust to correctly help you to identify which type of depression you may have and the best course of action and/or treatment that will work for you.

Major Depression, also known as unipolar or major depressive disorder, is characterized by a persistent feeling of sadness or a lack of interest in outside stimuli. The unipolar implies a difference between major depression and bipolar depression, which refers to a fluctuating state between depression and mania. Instead, unipolar depression is uniquely focused on the "lows," or the negative emotions and symptoms that you may have experienced.

Dysthymia, also known as Persistent Depressive Disorder or Chronic Depression, is a mild and chronic type of depression that causes a low mood over a long period of time usually for at least two years or more, and is accompanied by at least two other symptoms of depression. This type of depression usually has less symptoms than major depression. Those who experience dysthymia can also suffer from periods of major depression, which can sometimes be referred to as "double depression."

Postpartum depression is a type of depression in which the mother suffers after giving childbirth, anywhere from weeks to months after childbirth, usually arising from the combination of hormonal changes, psychological adjustment to motherhood, and fatigue. It also almost always develops within a year after a woman has given birth.

Seasonal Affective Disorder (SAD), also known as Extreme Winter Weariness, is a form of depression that emerges at the same time each year. With SAD, a person usually has symptoms of depression and unexplained fatigue as the winter season approaches with its reduced warmth, color, and the daylight hours become shorter. When spring returns and days become longer again, people with SAD feel relief from their symptoms, returning to their typical mood and energy level.

Atypical depression is usually a type of depression that is less well understood than major depression. This depression is a subtype of major depression or dysthymic disorder that involves several specific symptoms, including increased appetite or weight gain, sleepiness or excessive sleep, marked fatigue or weakness, moods that are strongly reactive to environmental circumstances, and feeling extremely sensitive to rejection.

Psychotic depression is a subtype of major depression that happens when a severe depressive illness includes some form of psychosis. This type of depression includes a mental state characterized by disorganized thinking or behavior; false beliefs, known as delusions; or false sights or sounds, known as hallucinations.

Bipolar Depression, also called Manic Depressive Disorder or Bipolar Disorder, is a type of depression in which symptoms can interchange between mania and depression. This type of depression has major highs and lows. The main difference between the unipolar and bipolar depression is that unipolar depression has no high periods.

Premenstrual dysphoric disorder, or PMDD, is similar to premenstrual syndrome but is more severe. PMDD is a severe type of depression that affects women during the second half of their menstrual cycle. Women with PMDD are often misdiagnosed and told that it's just hormonal and to get over it. Women with PMDD also have an increased sensitivity to their reproductive hormones during the two weeks before their period starts. This sensitivity leads to adjustments in the brain chemicals and neurologic pathways that control their mood and their general sense of well-being.

Whatever type of depression you have, it's always a great idea to try as hard as you can and find someone you can trust to talk to. It is very difficult to do every day things if you are in pain and suffer from any type of depression by yourself. Getting help doesn't always mean being locked up or being put on drugs. Sometimes, getting help just means having a really good friend who will love you despite of the obstacles that you face on a daily basis. It means having a friend who won't judge you, but one who will support you in your growth through that depression every single day. Depression is hard enough without having to battle other people's perceptions, thoughts, feelings, and ideas about you.

What Does It Mean To Be Codependent

What does it mean to be a codependent? A person who is codependent, also known as "having a relationship addiction", is a person who has an emotional and behavioral condition that affects their ability to have a healthy, mutually satisfying relationship because the relationship is one-sided, and they rely on the other person for meeting nearly all of their emotional and self-esteem needs.

A codependent will have low self-esteem because they feel that they are not good enough and always compare themselves to others. They constantly need approval of their self-worth from other people and when they don't have that, they feel unloved and inadequate to society. The constantly strive for perfection and feel guilty when or if they don't reach it.

Codependents have a hard time of saying no, mainly because they don't think that they have a choice. When someone asks them to do something, they don't have a lot of self-worth to stand their ground and say no because they think the other person will not like them or will reject them. If they ever do stand up and say no to someone, they get high anxiety and try to make up for saying no. They often put other people's needs above their own, sacrificing themselves to accommodate other people.

Codependents have extremely poor boundaries in general, but especially when it comes to their feelings, thoughts, and needs. They are always feeling responsible for other people's problems and their feelings which can become overwhelming when trying to deal with their own. Sometimes codependents can also be closed off and withdrawn so they don't get hurt. With poor boundaries, codependents can be very reactive like a grenade. They tend to be very defensive at times and very gullible at other times. Due to the lack of boundaries, codependents absorb other people's words, thoughts, and feelings like a sponge instead of realizing that everyone has their own opinion.

Being helpful is another huge thing with codependents. They are always trying to put other people's needs above their own. They always have to help other people, but if they ask to help, and the other person doesn't want or need their help, codependents are left feeling rejected, unloved, and unwanted. They will even try to "fix" the person or situation thinking that their relationship is broken and damaged just because that person doesn't need their help.

Shame and low self-esteem create a lot of anxiety and fear. These feelings are mostly about being judged, rejected or abandoned, making mistakes, being a failure, and/or feeling trapped by being close or being alone. This high level of anxiety and fear can often lead to feelings of anger and resentment, depression, hopelessness, and despair. Because they are so many feelings at once, the codependent becomes numb, learning to suppress emotions or push them into the subconscious.

Codependents can also be obsessive by spending their time thinking about other people or relationships and lapsing into fantasy about how they'd like things to be or about someone they love as a way to avoid the pain of the present. Alternate universes become muddled with actual reality. The idea of spending time in a "happy" world is more important than spending time with "real" people. With this obsessive behavior is the need to be "in control". This need helps codependents to feel safe and secure. This need is also accompanied by addictions of other sorts, such as, gaming, alcoholism, sex, drugs, gambling, etc.

I have been codependent for a long time. I have learned to control my environment, but especially when I am not able to, I play games. Games like Sims, High School Story, IMVU, Second Life, etc. Games in which I can create myself to look how I want to look like and to make my environment look like I want to make it look like are fun and important to me. They make me "feel" better even if only temporarily. In a world where I have pretty much no friends, I find that computers, and people in computers are my friends. Communicating with them is way better than communicating with people in the "real" world.

Watching people in the "real" world who I am codependent on, I realize that they may be a part of my world, but I will never be a part of theirs. I may share my feelings, hopes, and dreams with them, but they will never do that with me. I may want to invite them over my house, but they will never do that with me. If I have a problem, I share it with them, but they will never share their problems with me. I will invite them to my parties and other events, but they will never invite me anywhere. It is very lonely and depressing being a codependent…and I don't know how to change that.

What Is A United States Orphan

United States Orphan

/yo͞oˈnīdəd/·/stāts/·/ˈôrfən/

[yoo-nahy-tid] · [steyts] · [awr-fuh n]

noun

any child who was placed in the Department of Social Services' custody for at least a year, but was not adopted by their eighteenth birthday

According to the Children's Bureau (An Office of the Administration for Children and Families), there are roughly 400,000 children in the US foster care system. Of that number, approximately 100,000 are waiting to be adopted. According to ABC News, taxpayers are spending $22 billion a year — or $40,000 a child — on foster care programs.

Related Words: foster care, juvenile delinquent, DSS (Department of Social Services), CPS (Child Protective Services), group home, foster home, mental institution, respite care, homeless, teen shelters, kinship, ILP (Independent Living Program), judge, emancipation, ADD (Attention Deficit Disorder), ADHD (Attention Deficit Hyperactivity Disorder), CASA (Court Appointed Special Advocate), FFCA (Foster Family Care Agency), ISP (Individual Service Plan), abuse (can be physical, sexual, emotional, or spiritual), Jail Bait, noxious substances, RSP (residential service plan), aging out, caseworker, juvenile court

Fact or Fiction

- All children placed in social services custody go directly to foster care.

Fiction, when children get placed in social services custody, they are not always placed with foster parents. Some of the places a child will get placed include: group homes, respite care, temporary shelters, behavioral health center, mental institutions, with a kinship, or some may become homeless.

- A child is placed in social services custody because DSS have found sufficient evidence that they should be there. Once there, they are placed in a safe place away from all abuse until the parent is proven to be fit.

Fiction, there are a huge number of children placed in social services custody without sufficient evidence of abuse in the child's home. A lot of times, a parent will find that the only way that they will get a fair trial is in hiring their own lawyer. Such lawyer can cost quite expensive possibly starting out around $50,000 to $60,000 and up. Children in DSS custody are also sometimes placed in approved places or homes where they are being abused, whether physically or sexually, but have not been in their own homes.

Works Cited

Babbel Ph.D., M.F.T., Susanne. "The Foster Care System and Its Victims: Part 2." Psychology Today, Sussex Publishers, 3 Jan. 2012, www. psychologytoday.com/us/blog/somatic-psychology/201201/the-foster-care-system-and-its-victims-part-2. The Foster Care System and Its Victims: Part 2: Once placed in foster care, a child is not guaranteed safe.

Babbel Ph.D., M.F.T., Susanne. "The Foster Care System and Its Victims Part 3." Psychology Today, Sussex Publishers, 11 Jan. 2012, www. psychologytoday.com/us/blog/somatic-psychology/201201/the-foster-care-system-and-its-victims-part-3. The Foster Care System and Its Victims Part 3: An abused and compromised foster care system carries negative consequences.

Babbel Ph.D., M.F.T., Susanne. "The Foster Care System and Its Victims: Part I." Psychology Today, Sussex Publishers, 27 Oct. 2011, www. psychologytoday.com/us/blog/somatic-psychology/201110/the-foster-care-system-and-its-victims-part-i. The Foster Care System and Its Victims: Part I: Foster care is not always the safe haven it should be.

"Child Abuse Statistics (and the Best Resources)." INVISIBLE CHILDREN, Kids At Risk Action (KARA Group), www.invisible children.org/2017/12/29/child-abuse-statistics-the-best-resources /?gclid=CjwKCAjw1ZbaBRBUEiwA4VQCIUw0QAiCGfzA5-Fz48sXR9wdS14mD2fxxmxtJJhpAIubH_dytO-VcRoC8 _UQAvD_BwE.

"Facts on Foster Care in America." ABC News, ABC News Network, 30 May 2006, abcnews.go.com/Primetime/FosterCare/story?id= 2017991.

Friedman, Gordon. "Report: Foster Care in Oregon Is Getting Worse." Statesman Journal, Statesman Journal, 29 Aug. 2016, www.statesman journal.com/story/news/politics/2016/08/25/report-foster-care-oregon-getting-worse/89360654/.

"The Horrors of Foster Care Abuse Statistics." The Law Offices of Andrew Ritholz, 9 May 2016, www.ritholzlaw.com/2016/05/09/horrors-foster-care-abuse/.

Tittle, MSW, Gail, et al. Child Maltreatment in Foster Care: A Study of Retrospective Reporting. University of Illinois. Child Maltreatment in Foster Care: A Study of Retrospective Reporting; This project was supported in part by the Children and Family Research Center, School of Social Work, University of Illinois at Urbana-Champaign which is funded in part by the Illinois Department of Children and Family Services.

U.S. Department of Health and Human Services, Administration for Children and Families, Administration on Children, Youth and Families, Children's Bureau. "Adoption & Foster Care Statistics." U.S. Department of Health and Human Services, Administration for Children and Families, Administration on Children, Youth and Families, Children's Bureau (ACF), U.S. Department of Health and Human Services, Administration for Children and Families, Administration on Children, Youth and Families, Children's Bureau, 30 Nov. 2017, www.acf.hhs.gov/cb/research-data-technology/statistics-research/afcars. Preliminary FY 2016 Estimates as of Oct 20, 2017: No. 24. 'FY'refers to the Federal Fiscal Year, October 1st through September 30th. Adoption and Foster Care Analysis and Reporting System (AFCARS) FY 2016 data: AFCARS Report #24

Wexler, Richard. "Abuse in Foster Care: Research vs. the Child Welfare System's Alternative Facts." Youth Today, National Coalition for Child Protection Reform and Youth Today, 20 Sept. 2017, youthtoday.org/2017/09/abuse-in-foster-care-research-vs-the-child-welfare-systems-alternative-facts/. Abuse in Foster Care: Research vs. the Child Welfare System's Alternative Facts

Where Do I Belong

People look at me and they see an American. They see a person of color, a black person who is spoiled and has very little knowledge. There have been some Africans and Native Americans who have put me into the same category as all of the other Americans. America was not my first choice. I did not choose this country to be born in. I did not inherent this culture. I did not choose this language to emerge from my lips. I want to go home.

Home where my ancestors created, lived, and worked the lands. Home where nature is my friend and culture is in my blood. Home where tribes and villages are natural, and family is important. Home where education becomes second nature and hard work is common.

My culture, Blackfoot, African, and Creole is the identity that I claim. The country that I live in currently is America, but it is not my "home". I can't go home. I can never truly go home. It saddens me that I will never, never, never ever be able to go home. Sure, I can try and travel to Africa, Canada, Texas, and Montana, and visit cities, countries, and tribes and they may or may not accept me. Sure, I can try and learn the dialect, the languages, the culture, the daily life of the countries that my ancestors came from, but I will never ever, no really never ever be able to go home. That right there is the most depressing thing in the world.

Some of my ancestors were from West Africa. Cameroon, Congo, Bantu, Togo, Benin, each tribe in Africa had their own hairstyle. People of different tribes knew what kind of tribe you were from by the type of hairstyle you wore. A lot of tribes had their own language. Ewe, Fulani (Fulfulde/Pular/Pulaar), Soninke, Wolof, French, Adamawa, Senegambia, Serer, Igbo, Yoruba, Mòoré, Swahili, and Baatonum, such beautiful languages, but forever foreign to me. Europeans came in and shaved the heads of my ancestors. They beat their language into my people, took away their confidence, and broke apart their families.

Some of my ancestors were Blackfoot Indians. Very skilled hunters, artistic, spiritual, and warriors. They spoke Algonquian. When the Europeans came, they brought all of their diseases with them including small pox and measles which wiped out a significant percent of my Blackfoot population.

I belonged to my ancestors. I belonged in my home. Now hundreds of years after my ancestors were killed, beaten, and massacred, this so-called amazing country still hates the color of my skin. This so-called beautiful country still refuses to allow me to have confidence in myself and my culture. This so-called wonderful country keeps telling me that I will only become what they want me to be…and I am supposed to love every minute of it and say thank you for trying to survive.

Where Do I Belong? My history and identity, where is it? Where Do I Belong? In a country where hundreds of years later, I still fight for freedom every time I walk out my front door, or every time I panhandle on the streets in order to keep that front door. Where Do I Belong? I feel like my need to belong is stronger than it has ever been before. I am getting older and want to know more about where I come from. One of my uncles once told me that my biological relatives would be really upset if I kept digging into my past because some people don't want the truth exposed and want the past to stay buried. There are other people who tell me all the time that I shouldn't and have no reason to be depressed even though they don't even know me or even try to, but my question is still the same: Where Do I Belong?

An Alternate Universe

Our brain, connected by millions and millions of neurons, is as massive as the universe, if not more. We can hold huge amounts of information, process as fast as a computer, and think about things in an infinite number of ways. Most people do not utilize their brain's full potential. Damaged, the brain cannot fully repair itself. It cannot fully regenerate itself to last for centuries. It is one of the weakest and yet strongest parts of the body. Shake it too much, knock it around too much, feed it too much of the wrong thing, and the human brain can lose control, shut down, and even become nonexistent or useless.

I dare not dream in black in white, for color is all I see. I see trees and meadows, forests and oceans, and underwater caverns and places unknown. No, my brain never shuts off, especially when I am asleep. Being creative is great, but my brain never powers down. On top of being creative and having a brain that runs 24/7, I am also overly empathetic. If someone tells me their story, I can literally put myself in someone else's shoes, feel their pain, and even exhibit emotions because of that situation. I have learned over the years, however, how to limit my empathy very well and become numb.

Music is my brain's best friend. With music, I travel to faraway and unknown places. I have an alternate universe. In this universe, I am married to my "real" secret crush…a crush that I haven't been able to shake or break…a crush that I have had in "real" life for over a decade. He loves me. We have kids and I am happy with him. In this place, I am married to him there and I have a totally different life. I can hear my parents talking and giving me advice...parents who love me and don't try to control me. My father is so overprotective, and he keeps me safe. My whole family are prayer warriors. They make sure that they know that they love me and that I always have a home to go back to. These parents are "real" people, but in "real" life, they are not my parents….only in my alternate universe. I have a stable life. There is not a shortage of drama in my alternate universe, and sometimes, my real reality and my alternate universe collide. The difference is that my alternate universe always helps my real reality stay on track. Like being trapped in an endless movie, my alternate universe never ends.

Having two worlds can be very hard sometimes, but is also very helpful. There are times when I have just sat down in one spot listening to music and stayed in my alternate universe for hours. No one truly understands what that's like for me. It is healing and yet at the same time, very hard on my circumstantial depression to be in my alternate universe. However, at least in there, I have friends and family who love me unconditionally and not only when it is perfect or convenient for them.

Dealing with real reality is hard because it very depressing. My depression is based on my circumstances and the depression can end when the circumstances change, but a of times, my circumstances don't change, the evolve. The aftermath of these circumstances that I am constantly going through leaves me with tons of trust issues, high anxiety, paranoia, exhaustion, lots of stress, "dirty" issues (the feeling of being dirty all the time even after washing), loneliness, tiredness, and the need to keep my life balanced between "too much" work, and the right amount of fun and relaxation. For instance, there are certain times when I am not able to have constructive criticism in the "real" world because my daily allowance of what I can handle has been all used up by other people and especially my biological mother.

My daily allowance is a certain amount of negativity, constructive criticism, advice with negative connotation, negative words or phrases, etc. that I can mentally and emotionally handle in any period of 24 hours before I go through my "destress" process. I have to go through this destress process a lot and it is very important for me that I do so. My destress process usually includes a no negativity couple of days. I have called in to work before because I couldn't handle it. I stay in bed, listen to music, and only watch shows that are uplifting. There are certain times when I watch TV shows or movies who pull out my situation and allow me to cry everything out. Regardless of how everything comes out, the days when I cry the hardest and release everything, are the days when I have to use a washcloth as a bit in my mouth. The pain is so excruciating and always manifests itself physically. However, there are some days when I try to go through this destress process and all I feel is numb and can't cry...so I am unable to dump everything. Instead, I push it down and down and down until it randomly comes up in my dreams and my alternate universe while I am sleeping, and I wake up crying. When this happens, I know that I am going to have a bad day. Feelings are not like food that you got all over your hands and mouth....for me, I can't just shake or wipe it off and everything is fine. It doesn't work that way. Every day, there is a process, a very hard process that I have to endure.

After the destress release, I am usually very drained. The last thing that I want and need, is mentally and emotionally damaging people around me. I usually sleep a lot after a release. I also go very deep into my alternate universe and stay there for a long time. A lot of times, that's not possible.

When you rely on someone for financial, academic, or other kinds of support, they hold all of the cards. They tell you what you can and cannot do, think, feel, and how to behave. They control you. You are never free. With me, I have tried so hard to become independent, but it always seems like I just can't catch a break. For example, I get a job, then my car breaks down and I don't have the money to fix it or get another one. So, I end up losing my job. The only time I got myself off of welfare was when I traveled to a really big city in southern state. I worked for a particular company, had medical, dental, pension, and 401K. Then they decided to lay everyone off right after I got pregnant out of rape. I remember being six months pregnant thinking who would hire me now.

The real world is a very cruel place, but the loneliness, the loneliness will kill you. It is a haunting and vast emptiness that you feel makes depression worse. I never went to public high school, so I never received the same socialization that a lot of Americans experienced. In high school, I am told that, that part of your schooling is the foundation of your life. It's where you are supposed to develop your identity and communication skills, or some part of it. You also gain friends and necessary socialization and dating skills. I have been trying to figure out why I am unable to make friends since I was released on the streets by social services. People can say that it is better by yourself, but even the social experiment, Castaways, knows better.

I am surrounded by people who don't even know me because they don't have the time. One of my counselors that I had suggested to me that I should sign up for eHarmony in order to learn how to socialize. So, I did. I am on a lot of dating sites and have been for years, but they are boring because no one seems to want to talk to me. I try to put on a positive face every time I meet people, but after a while it just feels relentless and depressing.

My alternate universe became my 3D world. A world in which I internalize and see things in a whole new and different perspective. I can see and hear the faces and voices of those I wished were close to me and the faces and voices of those I don't want anywhere near me. My world where I am loved, appreciated, and surrounded by success. In this world, there are also disappointments, failures, depression, and negative circumstances, but in this world, the joys, laughs, and happy moments outweigh the bad ones. This world is my home. It never goes away, and it never will, and it is my safe and sacred and beautiful home.

The Thing About Being
Black In America Is

When you walk down the street, you can see the glares. This isn't the 60's, so you expect others to be understanding that you can't change your color, you can't change your race. You walk into a grocery store to buy some food. The manager stares you down until they make you feel like you shouldn't be there.

Other races say you are just imagining the overexpressed racism, but a whole lot of my race are saying the saying thing. The thing about being Black In America is that no one cares how much racism you suffer. No one cares about how much pain you are in when people hate you because of your race. If people hated me because of my attitude, that I can change. My behavior, my clothes, my choices, those are things I can change.

A white man walks into a bank with a gun showing in his pocket. He has a permit. It is legal to carry a weapon with a permit. He takes care of his business and walks out. The thing about being Black In America is that when a black man walks into the same bank with a gun showing and a permit, he is shot down seconds later with no questions asked because someone felt threatened or the "Stand Your Ground Law".

Malcolm X once stated, "The media's the most powerful entity on earth. They have the power to make the innocent guilty and to make the guilty innocent, and that's power. Because they control the minds of the masses." The media portrays all of these black people on TV in a very bad light. The media teaches America that black people are nothing more than gangsters, drug dealers, pimps, thugs, hoes, welfare hogs, etc. The thing about Being Black In America is there isn't a whole lot of media coverage on hardly any positive black people. You are more likely to be on TV if the media portrays you in a bad light than a good one.

The thing about Being Black In America is that a nation of black people are getting tired of hearing about Martin Luther King Jr.'s words, but all they see, and feel is hatred. Love is supposed to drive out hate. Kill them with kindness, and they kill you with their bullets. Hands Up, Don't Shoot leads to massacres. Turn the other cheek leads to women being beaten in front of their children by a sea of police. Believe that your life can be better only leads to thousands of black people still being paid lower wages in this country than any other race. It's not as bad as it seems feels quite bad when people are so scared of your race that would rather shoot you than actually carry on a conversation with you.

A Nation Is Crying!
A Nation Is Dying!
United We Stand,
Divided We Fall!
Black People Are Knocking,
Will You Listen,
Or Will America Fall!
Oppression, Depression,
Can Only Last For So Long,
Slavery Abolished!
Segregation Integrated!
You Can Kill Us,
But We Are Still Standing!

The Thing About Being Black In America Is, We learn from you! We learn hatred from our oppressors! We learn to fight to the death from our murderers who shoot to kill and get no jail time! We are not monkeys, we are human! We are watching you! We are learning from you!

The thing about Being Black In America Is, we didn't ask to come here...your ancestors ripped us from our heritage, our families, our lives, our homes. During slavery, when we tried teaching our children the value of family, you ripped that apart by raping our women and killing the fathers who didn't obey you! Our family values were trashed! Did you try at least to reteach us those family values when slavery was abolished?!!? Oh, that's right, it wasn't your job, but it was your job to tear those values down for years! Did you teach us Black History in school? Did you at least teach us what our heritage was when slavery was abolished? Did you do anything to make sure we knew how not to be slaves? Did you allow us to have a proper education? Did you raise us up to your level and say you were sorry? Did you teach us manners? Did you teach us anything besides hatred? I'm sorry, I guess that wasn't your job either! Oh, that's right, you segregated us! We became the scum of the Earth while your values and education continued to progress! I guess it wasn't your job to show us that we actually mattered to you. It wasn't your job to show us that our men were supposed to be the head of the household. It wasn't your job to show reteach us our culture, our heritage, our love for our families.

When we try to show our heritage now, you trash us and tell us it's unprofessional to be black. "Your hair has to be straight, no matter how much that relaxer damages your hair and makes bald spots in your hair!

You can wear tracks and weave even if you can't afford it if you want to work in our country! You have to talk white in a sea of us! We don't want you to stick out! Keep your heritage to yourselves, but we gladly are more acceptable to other Asians and Spanish Heritages! Don't say Black Pride or Black Power, even though it means to be proud of your heritage! We gladly accept Gay Pride every day! You can only have Martin Luther King Jr.'s Birthday as a national holiday! We gave you that one! Kwanzaa, Black Love Day, and Juneteenth are completely unacceptable! What did you really think you were American!"

The Thing About Being Black In America is, WE have been trained NOT to care about each other, so that way YOU could have an excuse NOT to care about us!

Generational Bonds
and Curses

Release these bonds that strangle me,
For the past five generations,
That's all I see.
From parent to child,
This slave behavior is an anomaly.
No dads around,
The woman an island,
The children the minions,
Society the oppressor,
Blacks the cattle,
Social Media the bit.
Self-confidence and self-esteem depreciating,
Failure always imminent,
The fight to stop segregation and racism keeps deviating.
They call this duck a cat,
And they call this cat a house,
I ain't black I'm American,
But these Caucasoid eyes still look at you,
Like you a Negro in comparison.
Repeating our ugly history again and again,
They indoctrinate their ways and culture like a louse,
Never allowing us to have or keep our own,
Making sure that we stay in their confined little monkey house.
Cops keep shootin',
And we keep sayin',
Yes Masta,
To a country that will forever,
Hate who we are,
And generational curses,
Forced upon us by our white slave lords,
Never to be forgotten in our subconscious little brains,
While they sit back and reap our hard-earned rewards.
The lingo we claim,
The culture we claim,
The hair we claim,
The clothes we claim,
The scraps we claim,
The attitudes we claim,
But if you really take a look in the mirror,

You just as colored,
As the other blacks you fail to claim.
And I guarantee you that if those Caukies got their chance,
They would shoot yo ass too,
That's the name of their game.
Babies having babies,
Put up for auction,
Each one of those blacks with a price on their heads,
That will forever be a part of America's concoction.
Generational Curses and Bondages,
Or Slave Mentality,
Actions speak louder than words,
So, let's see how yours compare to be.
So, release these bonds that diminish me,
For the past seven decades,
That's all I see.
From parent to child,
This slave behavior is still an anomaly.

Babies Raising Babies

Two Babies….two little girls that both came into this world in very different ways. Two very different labors, pains, pregnancies, doctors who delivered those babies. Two very different attitudes, perceptions, hopes, dreams, and experiences. Two beautiful children with such very different starts into this very hateful world…and I was their mother.

My oldest daughter was born October 31, 2001. Now, if I haven't told you yet, I was emancipated on the streets by social services around March or April 2001. I honestly didn't know that I could get pregnant. I was told by doctors that because of all of the sexual abuse that I had gone through that number one, they had no clue to when my virginity was taken, and two I wasn't able to have kids.

I had been in many different placements. Social services tried to put me back home with my biological mother and instead of she and I working on our relationship, she had another plan in mind, a girlfriend. Her girlfriend was more important than me or any kind of relationship I was going to have. I was suicidal and scared people, especially when I went to church. No one cared if I lived or died, so why should I.

There was one time, I went to a church and apparently, they were casting out some demon that was in someone. I just thought it was fascinating. The kids stayed in the sanctuary (which I now know that most churches do not do today), and I watched as they attempted to cast out this demon. I wasn't scared of demons and the idea that I actually got to see this process excited me.

My old church that I had gone to before being put into social services never reached out to me, so I just showed up. It was obvious that they were not really happy to see me. They didn't care. They said the casual hi, but I guess I was expecting something different…they hadn't seen me since I was a kid and that was five years ago. Now I have no idea what happened or exactly why. All I know is that apparently, I left with some man from the church and my biological mother was furious. She and this church had a huge argument. I don't remember why I left with this man, I don't even remember who this man was, I just remember that I just wanted to die and for someone else to pull the trigger.

This was a very dark place for me. I remember that I went to church with a couple and all I remember about that night is walking down the middle of the street and this couple trying to get me in the car to take me back to my biological maternal parent's house. I have pictures of that couple, but I don't really remember much about them either. I had already tried killing myself multiple times in different ways, but nothing worked.

I watched a lot of TV. There was nothing else to do. I didn't know anything about anything, and no one was trying to teach me. I didn't know how to be an adult, get a job, go to college, or anything. I saw ads on TV for an adult chat telephone line and I decided to try it out. Honestly, I didn't know what I was getting myself into. I still liked playing with barbies. The first guy I met, I remember going to the grocery store and getting stuff so I could make him dinner. After dinner, he just wanted my body. I didn't like any of it. He was rich and had I known better then, I should have just probably done whatever I had to, in order to stay with him, but I didn't.

Due to the fact that I didn't like the first one, I tried again. It's important to note here, that I didn't know what I wanted or what I liked. I didn't like any of this, but I didn't know what else to do all day. This was like a little dangerous hobby...a very bad one. Honestly, I really wish that I had someone to teach me something, but I never did. No one cared about me. Melva Cordell (this teenager I knew as a child who went missing) and my biological mother had always taught me one thing though when it came it men, they only want you to please them. Every situation I had been through up to this point, prepared me for this.

The second guy I had met, we talked on the phone for a second. Then my biological mother, her girlfriend, and I had dinner over his apartment. I don't remember much, but this much I do remember. While my biological mother and her girlfriend were over the apartment, we went into his bedroom. He gave me the tour and his closet was stacked sky high with pornos of all different kinds. I asked him what he wanted, and he said something like show me what you can do. I gave him head, and then my biological mother, her girlfriend, and I started to leave. Downstairs, I was putting something in my biological maternal parent's trunk, and he slammed my hand in the trunk. Now my biological mother's trunk, once it shuts, starts to close tighter automatically. They got my hand out, thankfully, but after we left my mom's girlfriend said that this guy did it on purpose because she saw the whole thing.

Long story short, I needed a place to live because shortly after my biological mother made a choice and chose her girlfriend over me. I was out on the streets, alone. It is important to note that I was still in social services' custody at this point. I called both guys. I don't remember what the first one said, but whatever it was, either didn't make me want to stay with him all that much or I was just really stupid and naïve and made the wrong choice. I asked him to take me to the second guy's place...I had called him obviously, and he was waiting for me when I arrived. I will never forget that the first guy told me to be careful because he didn't trust this other guy. He looked dangerous. I told him that I would be fine, and I began living with this other guy.

I had obligations while living with a grown man. This man was 30 and I had just recently turned 18. The sad thing is that when I met him, he was also a convicted sexual offender and was nationally registered. He had been officially registered two years before I met him. He had one condition, I please him sexually, and he would give me a place to stay. No problem. I had learned how to give oral sex at the age of about 7 by a teenager, then again at 8 or 9 by another grown man, and again later at the age of 11 by a 22-year-old man who was taking up residence in my house at that time. The problem with my oldest child's father, came in where he wanted to sleep with me and for me to like it. So, I had to watch pornos for that, but even then, I still didn't really like it at all and I had to fake it the rest of the time that I was in this agreement.

So, bottom line was, about a few months or so after that, I remember chain-smoking 15 cigarettes, but I don't even know if I was doing it right. I had decided that day that if Jesus wasn't going to kill me, then I would try and get Satan to do it. I don't know how I got money…I can't remember. I had enough money for an Ouija board. I was going to ask Satan to do it. That's when my Daddy told me, that I was pregnant. At first, I thought it was a joke….I know what the doctors had told me, but then I tried to prove it. I didn't tell this man, and I went and bought a pregnancy test.

I informed social services and they took me to a motel room and gave me their own test. That was the last time that I saw them. This man eventually got kicked out of his apartment because one of his many other girls wrote FU on his door. I was in the shower at the time they had the argument which apparently was about me. So, I became homeless again and pregnant. I tried getting help from social services, but they chose not to help me.

Again, I am skipping. I ended up meeting up with this man again and he had a new chick and said that I could stay there for a while. He was supposed to take me there, but because he was late to work, ended up taking me in his car way out in the middle of nowhere. I didn't have a license and didn't know how to drive. This man told me that he wanted me to stay in the car until he got off of work (which was about eight or nine hours) with no food or anything while pregnant. I argued with him and told him that I knew how to drive. I didn't know the first thing about driving or what even a GPS was. He told me to take the car, run some errands for him, and pick him up when I got off. So, I took the car and had a boom box on the right in the front seat...he had no radio.

I took off and started driving. Apparently, I had went the wrong way back to the city, but I thought I was doing great. There were these narrow country roads. I turned right down one of them because I knew I had to turn around. I also had to restart the music in the boom box. When I turned right again and tried to change the CD in the boom box at the same time, I crashed right into the opposite side of the road ditch. It was weird. My left arm felt like there was a worm in it racing up my vein. Some people called the cops and I tried to get out and walk. Those people stopped me and told me that I couldn't leave the scene of an accident. I didn't know anything.

Long story short, I got to the hospital and the cops asked me what happened. I told them the truth, but when they called this man, he told them that I had stolen the car. I told the cop this man was lying, and the cop believed me, but I was now under arrest and pregnant. I had never been to jail before. There are parts of this story that I will leave out for now, but I want to fast forward to 2003 where I was in a whole new city and state with my daughter.

I didn't know anything about raising a kid. I had been locked up in social services for five years and I could barely raise myself. No one wanted to help me. I was alone, scared, and very depressed. I just need a little guidance on what to do and how to do it, but what I found out was that people are mean and hateful and that was not what I had expected. I thought if I tell the truth, everyone will believe me, but that was never the case.

It is important to note that I am now going to college at this point and trying to raise a child. I went to this church for help. They saw me and instantly hated me. They lied to me, tricked me, used money I had gotten for college, and belittled me all of the time. I think the main reason I stayed because one I was codependent upon the worship leader, and two, because it was a church....aren't all churches supposed to be Christian?

Fast forward to my child was in social services custody and I was trying to get her back. This worship leader was on the opposite side and telling the courts that I didn't deserve to have my child back. She was also part of one of the biggest black families in the city. Powerful leaders had already told me that no matter what I had said or how much I told the truth, they would believe her not me because of who her family was.

I brought all the evidence that I need into court. I brought letters, phone and doctors records to prove my side, witnesses, and more. They had more than a few very different and complete opposite statements from this woman, no evidence to back up anything she was saying, and a whole bunch of lies. One psychologist who examined me, who had said good things about me, recanted after this woman and her family talked to him and stuff. In the end, I lost. They illegally took her away. I had kept a lot of the evidence, but in the end, everyone who knew this woman and her family, not only wouldn't hire me, but also the lawyers wouldn't even look at my case. I was blacklisted and the only thing I could do was leave the state.

This woman raised my daughter for a little bit and then she was given to be raised by her father and his family. To this day, my daughter looks up to her father and says that he is her role model. In this twisted world where a convicted sexual offender could be a little girl's role model, the thought makes me cringe. She hated me at first because of all the negative things her father told her about me and about how I abandoned her. I had proof that I didn't and sent her pictures of all of the domestic return receipts that I had sent her that were signed. The address label on those receipts even had a picture of she and I.

To this day, I communicate with her on Instagram. I had given her a smart phone twice, but each time she lost it, or it was stolen. For me, in order to really deal with the pain of losing my child, I had to pretend that she was dead. Technically, the little sweet girl that I once knew, is dead. I may never know the young lady who still holds my oldest daughter's name because she may never want to get to know me fully. I sent her a copy of my oldest book and I have one picture of her and her sister together. It still hurts that I never got to know her or raise her, and it always will. It's like a stake in your heart that you can't remove. I loved her more than she will ever know or care to know. The main thing that I learned from that was, that evil always wins.

My youngest daughter was born out of rape. I am not going to go into details because the part that I really want to focus on in this chapter is her primary schooling. The one thing about raising a dark child in a very racist area is that you have to really watch the child's self-esteem. When my youngest daughter went into kindergarten, the teachers and the principal kept talking about how she was getting into so much trouble. I decided to come and see for myself.

My youngest daughter has been in school since she was 18 months old. She is extremely smart. In kindergarten, she was the first one on the window for knowing all of her ABC's and her numbers up to 100. She was the only one for at least two to three weeks. So, when the school kept saying that she was getting into trouble, I wanted to see why.

I went in to observe her. The first thing I noticed is that my daughter raised her hand like she was supposed to, but while she was raising her hand, two or three kids were pulling on her arm and the teacher said nothing. They have these carpet squares that they are supposed to sit in. Each child in a different square. The next thing I noticed is that while sitting in these squares, one of the children starting hawking loogies in my daughter's square. My daughter started scooting back and that's when the teacher told her that she needed to sit back in her square. I told the teacher why she was scooting back....because of the loogies in her square. The teacher looked at me, rolled her eyes, and told my daughter to sit there anyway. Another side note is that here in The Pacific Northwest, this particular Elementary School has a lot of complaints from counselors, parents, etc. when it comes to people of color. They are one of the racist ones here. The only person who actually stood up for my daughter was the PE teacher. A boy kept hitting my daughter while standing in line in the gym. The PE teacher walked over to the boy and told him to stop. The boy shouted at the PE teacher telling him that he couldn't stop, and so the PE teacher made him sit down away from everyone and calm down.

I tried telling the principal, but she just diverted telling me that my daughter is taller than everyone else and that the other girls hate her. This principal was no help. I ended up moving her to a new school after Christmas break.

It is hard to protect your kids especially in a racist environment. Blacks in general are hated a lot by noncolored companions...not by all, but more than half. Not all white people voice these opinions and that is why actions speak louder than words. I encourage any parent who has a child of color to wear hidden cameras. That's the only way to prove hidden racism. The fact is that back in the day, parents were allowed to be parents. Parents would pop up in the back of the child's classroom and watch their kids misbehaving....then their kid would get into trouble. Kids had consequences for their actions, not all of this reverse psychology which definitely doesn't work on all kids. Also, there were a lot of FREE extracurricular activities. I ran track, particularly hurdles in third grade. Now everything costs an arm and a leg and the only kids who do it are the ones who can afford it. They have taken a lot out of schools and it's really not fair to the kids. Racist teachers get away with microaggressions, belittling kids, and being discriminatory because parents can't prove it.

Also, this company who we shall call Company A came to Company B and told us that a complaint about bullying cannot be held up in court unless the bullying can be proven to be a hinderance to a child's education. The problem with this is that when you have a complaint about the school districts, and the school's administrative team and the school board aren't doing anything about it, you are supposed to then go to Company A. Company A works in the courts, legislatures, and communities to defend and preserve the individual rights and liberties guaranteed to all people in this country by the Constitution and laws of the United States. Company B is supposed to ensure the political, educational, social, and economic, equality of rights of all persons, and to eliminate race-based discrimination. We are technically damaging our kids, and these are the kids who will run America very soon.

Another thing about my youngest daughter is that she doesn't mature as fast as my oldest. I took my oldest child to the movies at 3 years old and she was very mature. We went and seen the Incredibles. My youngest one, at 9, still has poor impulse control. It has been very hard being a single biological mother, trying to raise my youngest dark daughter with poor impulse control, trying to work, trying to find childcare, and raising her in a racist environment. People, relatives, and neighbors have said that they don't want to deal with her because she doesn't listen. Almost all of the parents in our current neighborhood have banned their children from even playing with her or even being near her. No one wants to deal with or even be bothered with her.

I put her in chess club and basketball, and she does really great. She is really helpful and gets mad when people don't want her help. She is friendly....a little too friendly. She is smart. I have had to fight for her every step of the way to have the equality that she sort of has right now. Her second-grade teacher kicked her out of her class. No one listened to me, no one even cared what I had to say. My daughter didn't go to school for almost a week because she didn't have a class to attend. I was railroaded and the school put my daughter in special education without my knowledge and then told me that I didn't have a choice but to have her in there. It has been a rollercoaster, but then I asked for her teacher to be changed. She has a new teacher, a new counselor, a new group of support.

While it is important to note that my daughter doesn't have special needs, she just doesn't have a normal life. Someday, I hope I can give that to her. I am still immature when it comes to me. I am also trying to raise a child and learn how to be an adult at the same time. It is hard. Setting boundaries with people and cutting people off has become easier especially since I don't really have many people around me anyway. My youngest daughter still likes to cuddle and while I am trying to deal with my sexual abuse trauma as well as comfort her, that is also very challenging.

If I don't have money for bills, I panhandle. I don't have a little sign like most people....no I have a really big sign that I made from a large paint stick for the handle, several medium paint sticks for the back, a large folded box, a lot of duct tape, and a fat red permanent Sharpie. I made sure that my sign is not only weather proof, but also sturdy as well. I keep it in my room in case I need it. The sign says, "Single Hardworking Mom In Desperate Need For Help". I have only used it once since I made it almost a year ago. I know that no matter what, I have to keep fighting for my child emotionally and financially and stay sane at the same time. I try to do things with her to keep her self-esteem high despite what other people think or say or do. It's hard because I work a lot....never making enough. Someday, I really hopes that both of my children know how hard I fought for them and how much I sacrificed, but if not, then I guess it won't matter. Until then, I will continue raising myself and my youngest child...alone.

No one raised me. There isn't this magical parenting book that is supposed to teach you everything you need to know about parenting. While the government continues to step into the way that parents are allowed to parent and give children more and more rights, other people are very critical of parents who are "different". If you are too immature, don't parent the way they think you should, people tend to get antsy. When parents have screaming kids in the grocery store, it's not like you can just give them a spanking right there or tell them to stop throwing a temper tantrum because they can't have whatever they want. No, you can't do that, and people just give you the "evil" stare and roll their eyes. It is hard enough raising kids with a partner, let alone having to do it yourself.

The problem is that normal things like how to do black hair, trimming your "bush", making friends, what not to do during your period, wearing bras, etc., I now have to Google or teach them as I eventually learn because I wasn't taught myself. Through life lessons, I have been learning some of them, but then there are a lot that I just really have no answers and have a hard time with my youngest child. It is hard because I am essentially growing up with my child as she grows.

No one comes up and asks you how they can help because they understand what you are going through....no that only happens on TV. If you do tend to pop your kids even just a little and people see it, they are so quick to call Child Protective Services (CPS). No one offers support to the struggling biological maternal parent, the just criticize, belittle, and diminish who she is. On top of that, no one suffers more than the Black Single Mother. For not only does she worry about all of this, but also the financial, racial, and societal burden that most of other races do not face.

White men already statistically get paid more than other races in the United States. Then white women are supposedly next. After that comes the black man, and then the black woman is last. Sure, you have the Hispanics, Latinos, and Asians all mixed up in there, but the fact that this country still has this racist issue between blacks and whites is ridiculous.

So, this issue with CPS. If a person called CPS on you and you are that single biological mother with no support, your kids will be put into a system where they will forever be irreparable. Now, there is that about 10% of CPS that does good work. I am speaking from experience of a child who was in CPS and as a biological mother who had their child ripped from her arms when CPS only had hearsay and no other evidence. I am speaking about the lost kids in the system who Diane Sawyer does documentaries on in which they are drugged on mind altering medications that doctors a lot of times would not give adults. CPS can be called by people who don't like you, by people who may not understand, and/or by people who are so judgmental and critical of your parenting that instead of maybe offering help, they think that your child would be happier in CPS, a place where majority of kids are physically, sexually, and mentally abused. No evidence needed and that has been proven. Kids who really do need to be taken aren't, and kids who don't need to be taken are. So as a parent, you think about every move you make 100 times over in order to find out the best possible way to get your child to be able to live until the age of 18, when they may want to be on their own, without them getting arrested, on drugs, and trying desperately to help them get good grades so they can make it into college, all while everyone is staring you down and judging your every move.

Yes, you try your best as a parent with everyone judging you, then you breathe when they make it into college just as the police shoot them down because they were black, or just as college sororities use the Paper Bag Test and kill them due to hazing, or just as they are slaughtered by a society that hates them for who they are. Parenting is hard, but no one has it harder than the Black Mother. Some of us were latch-key kids and had to raise ourselves, some didn't ask to be a biological mother and had the choice given to us, and some thought we were in love only for that man to just stick-it and leave....for that's what a lot of our men do. Instead of sticking together, we fight hard to put up walls, raise ourselves, all while trying to raise our kids. We are mere black babies struggling to raise others...the only difference is, that in today's society, kids now have just as much rights as the parents. Children whose brains are not fully developed can sue their parents, choose to stay at home and not do chores, and tell their parents whatever they want. If we continue this way, then they too, will be babies raising babies.

Lost Child

Were you ever misdiagnosed, placed in a mental institution, emancipated on the streets, and then thrown away by the government because you were not loved, needed, or were considered trash?

Being in social services custody was never fun. Some of the things that I learned while being in there was: how to hate myself, how to slit my wrist when I was feeling a negative emotion, how much people didn't love me, how to have sex with my own gender, how to make someone can make me pass out, how to raise the dead, and how much people only loved me out of obligation. There were those quiet moments that I found when I could that really intrigued me, but for the most part, being in social services is kind of like being in jail. While I have never been to juvenile detention, I was wrongfully put in jail while pregnant with my oldest child.

I went into social services custody at the age of 12 in August of 1995, the month before my 13th birthday. My biological mom had tried to convince me to behave because according to her, I was going to have a really big party. The truth is, is that I was kind of a nerd who had no real friends. The only people who really liked me were the random men who popped in my life at various times for sex. That's a different chapter.

Long story short, social services separated my sister, my brother and me. My sister and brother got to stay together, and I went somewhere else. My sister and I were placed in the same placement a little down the road in a group home, but once social services saw how overprotective she was over me, then they separated us again. My sister would always fight my battles. If someone was picking on me, she would tell them to leave me alone. When they made the wrong choice and thought that she was a little girl with too much mouth to be defending me, she beat them up. My sister was three years younger than me. The day they put her with me in the group home was awesome; however, after they took her away from me, I soon realized that I would forever be alone.

The group home that I was in was way out in the middle of nowhere. Long looking grass that looked like hay adorned the sides of the streets. You could try to run, but there was nowhere for you to go because the police would catch you before you even made it very far. That's how far out this place was. I soon became the rag doll in this place. I was sexually molested so many times that after a while, I didn't even care. No one cared about me. The staff members pretended to care, but I knew better. It was in this placement, I started my writing career. The director encouraged me to write and I did. The one thing that I loved about this place was going out at night out the back door. You could look up at the sky and see the beautiful blanket of stars fill the sky. It was so pretty. This place started the long journey of no return for me.

I have been sexually abused in a lot of the places I went to. One of the foster homes that one of the social workers tried to put me in, is where I first received my name, "*Jail Bait*". **Jail bait** is a term that I learned while being in social services custody. It simply means, any child who is under the legal age of sexual consent for having any kind of sexual engagement with an adult who, after enticing an adult, engaged in any form of sexual intercourse or other sexual behaviors with that adult, then goes to the police and call it rape. I was 13 when I received that name from social services.

Social Services placed me in all different kinds of places. When they finally placed me in a behavioral health center, it was different. I was able to do music, swimming, art, and outings. I really liked the activities, but not the people. I got beat up a lot. One of the places I was in, I got jumped by two girls who the staff allowed to beat me up while I was sitting on the toilet in the bathroom.

When you got out of control and angry, a 400lbs man came and laid on your back until you calmed down or until he felt like getting up. It always felt like you couldn't breathe. They also gave you shots of Vistaril in your butt cheek if you did anything, they had to lock you in the restraining room for. I don't know how much they were giving us, but it always made me sleepy. It would knock some kids out for hours. I even know that eventually some of the kids that I was with in there, would do something just to get a shot and locked in the restraining room. If they thought you were really out of control, then they would shoot you in the butt, then restrain you on the floor until you passed out, then strap you to the bed (usually hands and feet), and then roll the whole bed in the restraining room.

The restraining rooms that I remember had four white cinder block walls and one door on one of the walls. The door had a plexiglass or hard plastic small window in the top portion of it. The flooring was cold, and hard. If you started hitting the walls or if you were a female who took off your bra and tried to strangle yourself, then you were strapped down on the bed and shot with Vistaril.

I hated being in those places. It was a constant reminder of how we weren't wanted. They labeled all of us with something. If you had been physically or sexually abused even once, then you had PTSD. I was labeled with so many different things. Social services' solution was to drug us up and make us tolerable to the adults who had to constantly put up with us. We were regimented all the time. We were cattle in a world where they hated children. Different from boot camp, the places I was in were prisons for children. If they didn't like your behavior, they just raised the dosage on your medication or gave you a stronger medication. The counselors heard what you said in your sessions, but they weren't really listening. I was always depressed around Christmas time. Telling the counselors meant that they needed to help you with that by masking the problem and doping you up on drugs. Never mind the fact of why I was depressed....that wasn't very important. It's easier to drug someone than to fix the real problem, but I had an even bigger problem, the medicine that I was on was only making me fat, a mere 245lbs. I had never been a big child. I ran hurdles in 3rd grade and I was pretty skinny until all of the medication that I was on changed things.

I was released from social services custody, after five plus years of being behind bars, four white walls, or whatever, on the streets homeless and pregnant by a convicted sexual offender. I had no money, no job, no future, no life. I remember the day that I was released. Social services took me to a hotel room, administered a pregnancy test, and then left. That was the last time that I saw them. I found out from another social services in a different local city that I had been emancipated. I didn't know anything except how to be in a mental institution, behavioral health center, and or a psych ward...and now I was on my own.

After being locked behind doors, it was time to fly and I had nowhere to go and no one to turn to. I didn't know the first thing about living or even being on my own. I was lost. I felt like Jesus had taken me, as a little girl, to the middle of the forest and then just left me there. In this little dry patch with light shining down from the sky and darkness all around me, I was lost. Little did I know at that time, that I would probably never find my way out of that forest. For the next 18 years, I would prowl that forest in search of a destiny that I would never even come close to finding...and that is where I grew up...LOST!

Confessions of a Lost Soul

Things I Have Learned From My Personal Experience
of Living In the United States of America

S pinning ever so fast. Up, down, around, sideways. I feel like I am in a world full of hypocriticals and antisocials. People who don't talk to each other and look at you funny because you are socially friendly. A world where humans would rather have technological companions, mates, and friends than a real human connection. I feel lost in a never-ending cycle of oppression and depression. A world that runs 24/7 and that will never be satisfied until it has quenched its thirst for blood.

If you are homeless, people look down on you. If you are not homeless and don't have the latest trends and fashions, people look down on you. If you don't have sex, then testosterone won't date you. If you do have sex, then you're a whore. If you are underage and grown men like and prey on you, it's your fault…you just jail bait. If you are older and you date younger males, you're a cougar. If you are suicidal and/or depressed, then you need drugs, and lots of them. If you are a drug addict, then you are a junkie. If you can't control your kids, then you need them taken away. While your kids are in school, you have no control over what happens in the classroom. If you have kids and you discipline them, you are a bad parent, especially if you spank them. If you have kids who listen to other kids instead of you while they are in school, then you are a bad parent and are not paying attention to your kids. If you are a kid, then you don't want anyone telling you what to do, so you run away. If you have kids that have been taken away into the system, they will be physically, sexually, emotionally, and spiritually abused.

If you are black, then you are a thug. If you are black, you are not allowed to wear your culture, your nappy hair, your Africanism, your natural hair, your beauty. If you are Muslim, then you may wear your hijab or turban. If you are Jewish, you may wear your kippah. If you are darker than a paper bag, then you are not welcome in most places. If you are lighter than a paper bag, then you will have an easier life than most. If you are black in America, then you should not be called African or have African in African American. If you are black in America, then you should not have American in African American. United We Stand, Divided We Fall Only Applies To humans in America that are the color of or lighter than the chest and stomach of an American Robin.

If you are a single mother, people tell you that you should have never had a child if you couldn't afford it. It doesn't matter whether you had a child out of obligation, rape, being naive, or whatever the reason. People in this country judge parents left and right, but then give more rights to the children while taking away the parent's right to parent. It's hard enough trying to raise your children without everyone judging you on top of that. On top of that, being a black parent is even harder. Your children go to school with white children only for them to be bullied and discriminated against because of the color of their skin and the texture of their hair.

It is very hard waking up every day smiling and talking to people who don't care about you. You talk to them and they frown. You say hi and they look at you like you're crazy. You want to have a conversation and they don't have time. You want to go and hang out and you're being too needy. You want to give someone a hug and you must be gay. You want to be socially friendly and something must be wrong with you.

I learned very early on that because I didn't go to public high school, I would always be socially awkward. I used to love people way more than I do now. People have taught me to hate. Humans are their own worst enemy. I tried being nice to people and they make fun of you, laugh at you, be mean to you, label you, and even categorize you.

No one cares if I disappear for a week. The only reason anybody would ever notice if I was gone is because I have a child. People don't call me or even want to hang out. I can't even have a real conversation without someone trying to control me or put me down. I ask a lot of questions and I am considered ignorant. I don't ask any questions and I find myself lost.

While Chinese celebrate their Chinese New Year, Mexicans celebrate their Cinco De Mayo and El Día de los Muertos, Jewish celebrate their Passover and Hanukkah and Yom Kippur, Islamic celebrate their Ramadan, Wiccans celebrate their Winter Solstice and Samhain (All Hallows Eve), Hindu celebrate their Diwali, Christians celebrate Christmas and Easter, Black people and African Americans here in America are supposed to have their culturally specific holidays. Juneteenth, Kwanzaa, Black Love Day, Martin Luther King Jr. Day, and Black History Month are just the major ones to name a few. Majority of our history and inventions are already excluded from United States History textbooks. However, living here in America, I have learned that we are the all-inclusive group when it comes to our holidays. People of color are trampled underfoot every single day in this country (whether we know it or not) and we tend to be all-inclusive. We have nothing that we can really say is ours because of our all-inclusivity. Black people in major organizations and groups have told me that because of the area that I live in currently, blacks and African Americans cannot afford to have the stigma of being "all black" when it comes to their celebrations and events. They have told me that we need to be all-inclusive to all races.

In my experience, I have learned that black churches in the Northwest support church-related events and not black or African American ones. Politicians that are not of color do Gerrymandering, and purge black sounding names off voter lists, burn black churches, and give out written false information about when and how to vote. Black school children still get spit on, called niggers, bullied for their race by school faculty and students, and told by their teachers *"… am I going to have to bring my whip to school to make you behave"* and we want to be all-inclusive. This country has never loved, respected, or appreciated us, but we want to be all-inclusive. We can stand for the United States National Anthem, but America doesn't stand for the Black National Anthem and we want to be all-inclusive. If I went to work and called someone a white cracker bitch, I would get fired, but a white person can go to school and call a 2nd grader a black bitch nigger and nothing happens. The court systems telling black families that unless they can prove that bullying is a hinderance to a child's education that there is nothing they can do. Black children in kindergarten made to sit in loogies that white children hock up on the floor and we want to be all-inclusive. Black families getting letters from their neighbors telling them to move their nigger black assess the hell out of the neighborhood and we want to be all-inclusive.

I have learned that if your skin color is darker than a paper bag in America, that will get your ass shot, raped, beaten, slaughtered, and sexually molested and the people who did that to you will be get away with it and be praised and gain riches…except if they work for or under Disney. I have learned that Freedom of Speech only applies to people not of color. I have learned that I don't have the same rights as people not of color and other races have sex with white people to lighten their race. I have learned that no matter how many steps America takes toward equality for people of color, they will always take 50 steps back for every step they take forward… and we want to be all-inclusive. I have learned that if blacks and African Americans were united, we would prevail, but because we are all divided, we will always falter. The Reverend Dr. Martin Luther King Jr. said, *"In the End, we will remember not the words of our enemies, but the silence of our friends."*

Normal

I can't sleep. I left school right after my math class one day. I couldn't remember what my usual routine for Monday way. I went straight home. I missed my counseling appointment without even realizing it. I didn't feel like doing any homework.

Movies constantly played thru my head. Feelings constantly surfaced my soul. Surrounded everyday with feelings of loneliness, heartache, emptiness, stress, and more. My heart constantly searches for replacements in my life.

"Normal" to me is not allowing my feelings, emotions, and dreams to affect my life, sleep, behavior, everyday routine....but mine does. When I think of my Bishop and First Lady, I have dreams of them adopting me. I think of their family also being mine. I think of someone adopting my daughter while I heal with my Bishop and First Lady.....yet sometimes my daughter is with me. I feel like I am repeating the same cycles of my past, so I hide. I hide behind work, church, and time schedules. The more time I spend at church, the better I seem to feel. I know that is because I am around my church family there. I don't get burned out because being at church, around all of the people who love me is my drug. If anything, I just want more. They make me feel safe, secure, loved...but they have families in which I am not a part of. They go home to them and they go to events and stuff with them. Is it normal to feel jealous of their families, of the love they give them? No, it is not normal...it is obsessive. It is draining to those around me. Like a leech, I suck the life and love of those around me. I tell myself, it's just because I have missed them, but I know better. I know the truth.

"My issues are on the outside, while other people's issues are on the inside." That was told to me by a Pastor who kicked me out of his church. Maybe, this was the reason. Not everyone can handle leeches. So much so where I have stayed in my car for long hours playing movies in my head. Movies that can last for days or weeks, the same movie can continue for a while.

I want to be able to heal completely from my past, so it doesn't affect my relationships or way of life. Sometimes like this long sleepless night, my sleep gets interrupted and I can't sleep. I wake up depressed because I am trapped in an endless cycle that won't end. Sometimes I think it would all be so much easier to just go back to an institution where I don't have to worry about anything. I have tried so hard to be "normal" and I feel like I am lacking all the time in that area. I can't go back, but it seems like I can't move forward. Codependency urges me to distance myself from others because I feel like I am too much for anyone else to be around. I feel like they hate me for needing them all the time even though I try really hard not to. What does a "normal" and "healthy" relationship look like? I talk to my "friends" on the computer. The internet is where they live. I have no friends outside of this computer, this social and digital environment. No one wants to be around me. So, I talk to my digital friends, whether real or fake, they are listening inside my computer.

All I want to do is cry because I am in pain. Pain from knowing that my life will forever be changed by my past, pain from knowing that I will never have the kind of life that is happy and free. What's wrong with me? Why can't I just get better? I think about hypnotherapy. I want to forget my past and be reprogramed. I have tried to brainwash myself. Overlaying messages with song tracks. That didn't work either.

The loneliness is overwhelming sometimes. I can't just climb under a rock and die because I have my daughter and she needs me. She really needs me to survive. I want to do right by her. I feel like I suck the life out of relationships around me.

I want to get better. No one understands when I say that I have been dealing with this since I was 18 years old, that it's true. Medication is for chemical imbalances; in which I don't have. I need to learn how to heal from my past scars, not mask them. My scars are like wounds that are bleeding. Every time I see it bleeding, I put a new Band-Aid over top of the other one. I have so many Band-Aids that the blood has begun to seep through all of the covered bandages. The Band-Aids aren't holding the wounds together anymore. I have been desperately trying to put more bandages on top, like someone who is trying to save a loved one from dying when they realize that the person they love is lying on the ground and losing to much blood. They try desperately to put pressure on the wound to stop it from bleeding. I am trying to save myself from dying mentally, physically, sexually, and emotionally completely.

No one can fix me. I know that it going to take Jesus for that. Doctors sometimes see miraculous things happen all the time in medicine. So, I know that Jesus can hear me. I am screwed up, messed up, and I need help. Counselors don't see what I see, feel what I feel. I have prayed many times for Jesus to heal me. I have seen many counselors throughout the years as well. I need to feel sane, whole, better than I do now.

In my head, I have learned how to be around Bishop without my sexual abuse affecting me. When I snap back to reality, I realize that I haven't healed from anything. My dreams feel like another Band-Aid. They make me laugh, cry, happy, sad. They bring me joy and pain, but they aren't real. In my world, I am healed from my past pain. I am free. I am rejuvenated. I am happy. I am a new person. I am at peace. I am helping others to grow and heal and flourish. I am "normal".

I Brought You In This World... I Will Take You Out

Mother, father, step or biological, foster, grand, aunt, uncle, sister, brother...parents and guardians are made up of all different kinds of titles. They can be extremely older than you, or very young. Who you were raised by does in fact have a huge impact on your life whether you want to admit it or not.

I lived with my biological mother until August 1995. I tried to run away because things were tough, very tough. My siblings and I had been tied to daybeds and beaten with broomsticks on several occasions. We snuck into the ice cream one time, because we were hungry and my mother made a concoction which was ice cream, salt and pepper, hot sauce, and I am not sure what else was in there....and made us eat it. My sister threw up, I didn't. When she went to work, my sister and brother were padlocked in the upstairs bathroom and I was in my room downstairs with a bucket to use the bathroom in and a roll of toilet paper. At least my siblings had the bathroom. We also were already equipped with our meals in those rooms until my mother got back. We were like cattle.

The month before I turned 13 years old, I tried to leave. My biological mother claimed that if I had behaved enough, that she would throw me a huge birthday party in our basement. She didn't seem to care that I was a nerd who got beat up a lot. I was the school's punching bag. When I was starving at home, kids at school who give me food that they had previously spit in. I was so hungry, I didn't know...but they made sure the whole school knew about it right after I gobbled down the food. Hardly anyone really liked me. So, how in the world was I going to have a party without any friends? In August 1995, I tried running away from home with my brother but got put into social services custody the same day. To this very day, my biological mother blames me for everything and says that, that entire situation was my siblings and my fault. It didn't matter about her tying us down to daybeds and beating us with broomsticks or locking us in the bedroom and bathroom until she got back from work. No, everything was our fault.

My biological mother could talk a very good game. She was the master of manipulation. When a police officer pulled her over, she begged, pleaded, and/or cried herself out of a ticket. When something needed to be sold, she could sell the shirt off of her back. Yeah, my biological mother was the master of manipulation alright, and she manipulated her children all the time.

As an adult, it is very hard for me to have my own personality or responsibilities. I get blamed for a lot of stuff that is wrong in my biological maternal parent's life. "If you hadn't done such and such, then things for me would've been different". When I had kids, I wanted things to change, but they just got worse. It doesn't matter what the situation or circumstance is, I am not allowed to say no to my biological mother. If I do, then I get asked why I am treating her like one of those people on the streets. I was not allowed to express how I feel. My biological mother never listened to me. She constantly tells me that she deserves to be respected because she is my biological maternal parent. I am not allowed to have an opinion or a standard or a set way of doing things because she knows how to live life better than I do. I started to tell her yes to things and then I just procrastinated in doing them. Then she tells me that I don't ever listen to her. My biological mother would say everything she had to say and then when I tried to express how I felt, she would cut me down and make sure I knew that I needed to trust her and stop arguing with her. I soon learned, after so many yelling matches, that it was best just not to say anything to my biological mother while she was speaking except yes ma'am or okay. It didn't really matter what my next move was, but my biological mother was the one who needed to be validated, not me. Whatever she was saying was more important than anything I would ever say. This began happening in other relationships throughout my life, especially at church.

I felt caged and locked in a world where I was better a mute than a socialite. My biological mother very rarely apologized. When she forced me as an adult into prostitution, her reasoning was that I wasn't able to find a job and so I need to bring money in by any means necessary. She claimed that she had been doing it for years, so now it was my turn. I saved up my money, bout a train ticket without telling her, then left two days later. I told her the night before I left that I was leaving. It didn't matter where I was going, I just didn't want to be around her. The difference is that when you have children, those children can be taken away if you are homeless.

I had my youngest daughter out of rape and my biological mother called my daughter a demon seed. My biological mother tried to force me to have an abortion with my oldest, but I managed to escape that....but she never lets me forget it. She always reminds me that she told me to have an abortion, but I don't listen to her. She did tell me that if I have a third child, she would punch me in the stomach and make me have an abortion like she did my aunt.

I set a bedtime for my youngest daughter and that's not happening because what she has my daughter doing is more important than the standards that I have for my child. I tell my daughter not to talk to strangers, but my biological mother tells her it's okay because she is sitting right there. I tell my daughter not to fight in school and to tell the teacher or the principal, but she tells my daughter if someone hits her hit them back.

I can never win with my biological maternal parent. I had to live with my biological mother for a while as an adult. My biological mother would clean the whole house before anyone got anything to eat, including my daughter. "She'll be alright", was the key phrase my biological mother always said. I would sneak my daughter a banana or something to eat. When my daughter wasn't allowed to go to bed at her bedtime for whatever reason, my biological mother would fuss at her that she better not act up in school. I knew that my daughter would though because she only got around 4 or 5 hours of sleep on a school night.

When I got my own place, I knew that things would be different, but they weren't. I got manipulated into giving my biological mother a key which was a big mistake. I had to try and figure out how to get it back or have the landlord change the locks. My car broke down, so I needed my biological mother to take my daughter to daycare. I told my biological mother that my daughter's bedtime was 7:30pm because my daughter needed her sleep and had to get up at 5:30am. My biological mother would pick up my daughter, run errands, do everything she had to do, then bring my daughter home. I knew then that my biological mother would never respect me as an adult. I had to figure out how to cut my biological mother off for good, but that wasn't going to be easy.

Unfortunately, I was scared of my biological mother at that point. We have fought before. She has punched me as a child and as an adult. One time my biological mother showing off photos of me when I was a teenager and 236lbs. I hated those pictures, so I took them and hid them. She got really mad and that was the very first time I had ever bruised. My bruise went all the way from the top of my neck and down to my side.

When I was in my thirties, she told me she was coming over to my apartment to get some of my DVD's for a little seven-year-old boy and I told her no. We argued because she was telling me what I was going to do, and I was trying to assert some boundaries. I thought that she would hit me again because I blocked her from coming into my apartment. She called me selfish. She said that I needed to have her back through thick and thin no matter what and that when she asks me to do something, I should do it no matter what without arguments. She said that she is my biological mother and that saying no was totally disrespectful. She told me that she was explaining to me what type of person she was and what type of daughter she is trying to have. She told me that she is not asking me to do anything wrong or go above and beyond any reasonable expectations. She left angrily. She also fixed my car one time, even though I told her she didn't have to. She told me that I needed to get out of her car, but I told her that I would figure out other transportation options. I had decided to stop driving her car, but she keeps insisting that it is necessary and that she doesn't complain because she is the parent and that's what parents do… sacrifice for their children. It is hard to stand up to my biological mother, but I keep trying.

The thing about my biological mother is that no matter how old I get I have no opinions, no right to say anything, no independence, no choice in anything. She tells me to jump, I am supposed to say how high. I am really trying to be independent. She asked me for a key to my apartment. I originally lied and said that I didn't have a second key, but she figured it out and kept giving me the guilt trip every time she saw me. If I don't answer the phone on the first ring, then I am the bad one….even if I am in a doctor's or counseling appt. My mom would call over and over again until I answer the phone. Then she would leave me a message saying she doesn't know why I never answer the phone and that she doesn't know why I treat her like a stepchild and that I am being so disrespectful.

Sometimes, I try and do things so I don't have to be around her. It is very hard being around someone who doesn't understand my depression or me. I work very hard to try and be independent. Financial independence is very difficult, especially right now. I always feel bad about myself when I get around my biological mother. She doesn't understand anything I try and tell her. In my former years, I had tried to tell her that I was suicidal, and she said if I wanted to kill myself then I should just do it and stop playing around. I can't really talk to my biological mother. She is very black and white, and I have no opinions and am not allowed to have a say so in a lot of stuff. When she needs to talk, I am her counselor.

In 2018, my biological mother and I went out on our first lunch date ever. I had to schedule the date on a holiday and kind of persuade my biological mother to go with me. She told me that she didn't want to go out to lunch with me because I am always picking my nails and other stuff. I explained to her that I do that at home, but that she didn't know me and has never been out to lunch with me ever. We went to a restaurant. It was very nice. She didn't criticize me or talk down to me. I made sure I paid for the whole thing. That was a very good day. The food and the conversation were great.

For my biological mother's 50th birthday, I made sure that I planned the whole day…that was when my car was working. I took her to iHop first where she had breakfast. Then I took her to get a full body massage at Jasmine Foot Massage in Tualatin, OR. They do amazing reflexology, deep tissue, and Swedish massages. I took my biological mother here because she does construction and has knots in her back. From there, I took her across the street where she had a full manicure and pedicure. Then we went out to eat and by that time, we just hung out with family at the a major City Park which is located beside a big City Library. I made sure she had a very great day. When my biological mother is having money spent one her and is not being loud and overbearing, she can be quite pleasant.

Someday, I hope that I can make more money than her so I can pay for her to have her own house 300 miles away from me. We would still talk and communicate, and when I would come and visit her, I would make sure that I stay in a hotel room…even though I would be paying for her house. I like my biological mother when we are 300 miles apart from each other. She is much nicer and not so overbearing. She and I cannot live in the same state though. I need to be able to be my own person without her in my space and constantly telling me what to do.

It is very hard to have an emotional attachment to a parent who you weren't raised by. I get it. For those who have been adopted, those who never knew their biological mother or their father, those whom the parent knew them, but because of separation for whatever reason, the child has forgotten them, I understand what it is like to not have this so called "love" for that absent parent(s).

My biological mother, the absent parent, tried to control me because she said that she's the parent and I should respect her no matter what. Whenever I had an opinion, it would get shut down and I wasn't allowed to voice it. She was my biological mother and I was supposed to respect her no matter what the circumstance or situation. She was giving me financial support and I, out of feeling obligated, was giving her moral and emotional support. The truth is, that until I finally set myself free from her financial support, I would forever stay trapped under this stressful control. So, I let her go, and everything financially that she held over me.

I had to argue and fight with my biological mother just for she and I to go out to lunch together. She told me that she and I can never hang out because we are different and don't see things the same way. She refused to spend time with me unless it was under her terms. When she was in my car, I could only listen to black music, not that "white" stuff.

She refused to accept me the way that I am. See, to her, I am brainwashed because I don't show and/or wear my culture 24/7. I love Christmas. Who cares where it originated from? I don't. I just want to be free to be me and have my biological mother love me for who I am…but she won't, she never will. I don't fit into her tiny little box. I don't listen to her every will and command. I am not her robot, and so unfortunately, I had to let her go. I had to say goodbye to her financial hold over me, goodbye to my obligations that I have for her, goodbye to the way she treated me and the way I treated her…and I cut her off completely.

No, you don't have to spend time with me…ever. No, you don't have to listen to my Christmas music every time you get in my car. No, you don't have to keep telling people how you financially help me to survive and how I am hard headed and don't listen even though I don't even know you. No, you don't get to keep taking my things because you feel like you have the right to do so. No, you don't get to tell me how to dress and what to wear and that you can't stand the way I look and so I need to go and change…even at 36 years old. No, you don't get to tell me that I am not "black" enough and explain to my child how I am brainwashed. No, you don't have to worry and stress over me at all, because you are no longer in my life. I don't even know you. Mom, what is my favorite color, and mom, what do I like to do for fun, and mom, what is it that I aspire to be in life, and mom, what do I fear when I am at home alone, and mom, what do I feel are my strengths and my struggles, and mom, what do I want for me? Can my biological mother answer any of those questions honestly without Googling them? Can any of the people in my life who call themselves my family and my friends really tell me that they know me? I have tried for years just trying to get my biological mother to see me, to accept me for who I am, but at the end of the day, she refused to accept me because it wasn't in her power to control me and she refused to see me. I asked myself why I still hold on to her and my answer was due to financial help. That is no reason to hold on to anyone and at the end of the day, whether I sink or whether I swim, I will do so because I did it on my own, not because my biological mother did or did not help me.

Do I love my biological maternal parent? Do I really love my biological maternal parent? I am not sure. I don't even know what love is anymore. Did I ever know what love was to begin with? Probably not. The bible says, in 1 Corinthians 13:4-8, that love is patient and kind. It does not envy or boast and is not proud. It does not dishonor others and is not self-seeking or easily angered. Love keeps no record of wrongs and does not delight in evil but rejoices with the truth. It always protects, trusts, hopes, and perseveres. Love never fails. I still am trying to understand what that means, not only as a woman, but especially as a black woman...and not only as a black woman, but as a single black mother myself.

Learn To Be Lonely

For as long as I can remember, I have never really had any friends. In 5th grade, I got beat up for being "white". I was called an "Oreo" (someone black who talks and acts white), nerd, and ugly on numerous occasions. I never remember having any play dates, parties of my own, or even being invited to any parties. For my birthday every year, since I think the age of 18, I have thrown my own birthday parties. I never spend less than $200 for food and $200 for decorations. People always showed up to eat and celebrate, but I was never materialistic, and I just wanted them to show up for me even if I didn't have a party. I just wanted people to spend time with me.

So, my aunt's birthday is the day before mine, so one year, I decided to combine both of our birthdays at a restaurant. My aunt knew about it and I sent out invitations. When people showed up, they brought her gifts and cards. I ask them where mine was at and they said that they thought that I was throwing this party for my aunt. I was happy for her, but sad for me. No one bothered to read the invitation, and no one really cared about me. If they did, then they would have listened to me. I am like a ship passing in the night. I am here, but most people don't see me.

I would love to have friends or people to celebrate with. Birthdays, graduations, funerals, holidays…celebrations where I celebrate with them and they with me. I would love to have conversations with people about how they are doing and catch up on what's been going on or shooting the breeze. I was told a lot by many different people that most people build the foundation for relationships and communication skills in high school. Some people even have friends that they still talk to that are from their high school years. So, because I didn't go to high school, what does that mean for me?

Sure, I love hanging out with myself too. No one talking during the movie, or smacking and acting "ghetto" in the fancy restaurant, or even gossiping about the other church members when you really just want them to have a decent conversation with you that shows that they want to really get to know you.

The truth is, I am not an antisocial. In this world I have found that it seems like everyone else is. When you ride the city bus, train, or subway, it seems everyone is in their own little world with their personal electronics. Headphones, mp3 players, iPod's, iPhones, and other Apple products align almost everyone's ears and faces now when you see them. Say hi to someone and they give you the "evil eye". There just doesn't seem to be friendly conversation anymore.

I go to church where everyone gives you a friendly hug and greeting. They ask you how you are doing, but they don't really want to know. The cultural mannerism in America to say "fine" or "okay" when asked that question has become tedious. In church, the response is usually "blessed" or "soul saved and sanctified". When I ask people if they want to hang out or go for coffee or to the movies, their answer is usually the same…they're too busy. Seeing their group pictures plastered all over Facebook where some of the women went to the movies or an event together, but didn't invite me just makes me feel like an outcast. When I ask them why I wasn't invited their excuse is the same every time…."it was a last-minute thing" or "I didn't plan the event" or some other excuse. You would think that after 3 years, I would just stop asking.

There are those other times when I have gone to an event and seen a bunch of my church members there and I go to say hi and they give me that look of "dang, there she is again". The last event I went to, I finally got it. I will never ask again. I think I finally get it when people don't want me around. Like the *Home* movie, when OH finally realized that people didn't like him, I feel the same way when I see people at church. I finally understood that you go to church to put on your "face". You pretend like everything is okay because church people quote the scriptures about take it to Jesus and not showing what's wrong with you. Relying on Jesus is the only way to make you happy. I always wondered why my Daddy didn't stop those men from raping me. The first time or the second, but what about the third or the fourth, why didn't he stop them from hurting me? I have heard some pastors and Bishops speak about how lonely being a Christian really is. I am not talking about having people around me all of the time, but it would be nice to maybe go hang out with someone once a month, even if it isn't the same person every month. My computer, my television, and my cell phone have now become my best friends.

Sims Free Play, The Simpsons Tapped Out, High School Story, Plants VS Zombies 1 and 2, Candy Crush, Farm Heroes Saga, Cookie Jam, Toy Blast, Spades Plus, Pet Rescue Saga, Disney's Magical Dice, Snoopy Pop, Parcheesi, Sonic Dash, Game of War, Forge of Empires, Virtual Villagers, IMVU, Virtual City Playground, Frozen Free Fall, Supermarket Management, and Survivors: The Quest, are just some of the games that I play on my devices. I have an iPad, a HD TV, iPod Shuffle, a Roku device, HP Pavilion Multimedia PC, Samsung Galaxy S6, and a 15-inch MacBook Pro. Even with all of the devices that I have, I would rather have people to hang out with than a whole bunch of electronics.

I have tried making friends in college also. I got a whole lot of numbers, invited them to events around town, and even tried to connect throughout and after college. They too are always too busy. I missed out on the joys of high school. So maybe, there is little hope for me as an adult. Trying to get to know people is like pulling teeth. People spend time with their families and close friends, but new people aren't allowed.

Here in the northwest, drinking is everyone's thing. Everyone is always going to a bar or an event where there is lots of alcohol. I remember when I first came up here and I thought that the northwest was full of a bunch of drunks. I couldn't find hardly no events that had zero alcohol at them. Being a single mother, sometimes I wanted to take my daughter to free events…ones where there were no alcohol present. It's sad that people feel like they can't have fun unless they are drinking alcohol with the activity.

In my apartment, I have a huge bookshelf full of board games. Splendor, Monopoly Empire, 7 Wonders, and Battle of the Sexes are some of my favorite games. I used to love going to game night that they have at some of the churches over here, but being a single mother is hard when you have no childcare and there are hardly no children at those events. I used to take my youngest daughter with me until she started stealing money out of the donation cup. I could talk about that situation now, but I will leave that to another chapter in this book. I no longer attend game nights and all of the board and card games that I have sit on my shelf collecting dust.

I think being lonely has somehow contributed to my sudden crush on Luke Cage, not the cartoon in the comic books. I started watching the TV show and I just started dating him in my own head. I still to this day have not seen Black Panther or A Twist In Time yet. I couldn't afford to go to the movies when they came out and they haven't appeared on Netflix or Hulu yet, so for now I love watching Luke Cage. Empire, Star, Law and Order SVU, The Crossing, Beyond, Wayward Pines, The 4400, The Returned, CSI (all of them), Once Upon A Time, Greenleaf, Queen Sugar, Beat Shazam, Grimm, Celebrity Family Feud, Being Mary Jane, For Better or Worse, Bring It, True Blood, Black In America, Extant, Unforgettable, Boy Meets World, Moesha, Beauty and the Beast, Bones, Under the Dome, Scandal, How To Get Away With Murder, Beyond Belief: Fact or Fiction, Beyond Reality, 1-800-Missing, Without A Trace, 911, Wheel of Fortune, The Million Dollar Pyramid, Cake Boss, Say Yes To The Dress, Pimp My Ride, The Walking Dead, Meet The Manns, Living Single, The Cosby Show, Girlfriends, 227, Amen, Showtime At The Apollo, and One on One are just some of the TV Shows that I watch.

As I watch the clouds crawl across the sky, the days turn into nights, the seasons roam by, and the years fade away, I ask my Father, "What is going to happen to me?" What will happen to me? I have employment specialists trying to find me a job and a peer support specialist who only helps with employment support and a counselor who is strictly professional. My heart yearns for people around me that I can just be myself with. Church people who see my, but don't really "see" me. They always love you when you are at church and working in the church, but when you are just a member sitting in the pews and seeing them come in and go out, it's as if time fades and the sun is like dust. It's all happy when you are at church and fellowshipping, but that's all it is every Sunday, the same routine, the same 'see you next Sunday', the same 'hugs and kisses', the same 'holy ghost filled dances', the same praise and worship, and the same superficial relationships. How many of them know me beneath the surface? How many of them even care?

I feel thirsty and starved for human connection and I feel like I am dying emotionally. Is it wrong for me to want to feel connected? I am not allowed to curl up and hibernate inside of my apartment. See, I don't have that luxury. I see people all the time on those reality TV shows who are enabled by people and curl up inside of their place and then Iyanla Vanzant comes in and saves the day with her philosophy, but sometimes despite what I hear her say, I can say how much a lot of her stuff to me feels like entertainment. The physical pain that I feel because of my depression and the lack of friendships and human connection that I seek even though I have tried a million times to make friends and the tears that I cry and the tears that I feel but won't come out feels like death. I sometimes have to put a folded-up washcloth in my mouth when I cry due to the amount of physical pain that I feel, and I sit in my bathroom and wonder why did God save me in DSHS custody just for me to go through all of this pain? I try to make sense of what it is and what I will become in the next year because Lord knows my life changes every year and I can't even think anyway of a stupid 5-year plan because my life is like a tectonic shift.

I go on interviews confident and well-dressed seeking white people's approval of my long straight hair, and my well-dressed outfit, and my well-mannered and 'white' attitude, and my put together attitude, and my put together personality….but then I get these letters saying they found someone else. Even going back to these places and seeing the type of people they put in that position, a white woman with nice pale or peach skin with long hair and sometimes short, with a skinny or even fat waist, with well-manicured nails and the lipstick to match…and I feel like a sack of trash that just got thrown out. See how I can develop relationships at work if I don't even have a job. Here in The Pacific Northwest, you cannot find 10 companies where a black woman is the face of the company, the receptionist, the secretary, the first person you see when you walk in the door. I am not talking about the janitorial staff or the security guard, I am talking about more than that. Then I take a look in the mirror and think to myself, 'how can I compete with that'? I even made it past the front door at one company, and I did everything they asked of me, even things that I didn't know that I could do. They hired me and filled out my employment verification for social services. I thought I was finally getting off of welfare and then after two weeks they told me that they decided to hire someone else. I went back a little while later to see the same thing, white person with great features. I learned that I am not accepted anywhere, not at church, not at school, not at work, nowhere. I volunteer lots of places, see everyone wants you to do a job for free.

I noticed while teaching art to kids at an elementary school that all of the school's staff is white, except the janitorial and kitchen staff and the playground teacher. I thought to myself, 'why do white people constantly try and push black people only into certain positions'? This isn't the first school that I noticed that, but at least this school had black janitorial and kitchen staff. There are some schools here that I have been to with only whites and Hispanics and Latinos. See when you first walk into a school, there is a huge frame on the wall....usually in the office area, that contains pictures of all of the staff for the whole school. You can always see if there is any diversity within the faculty of the school from that picture. I learned that even though white people hate me, my own race does too. Hispanics and Latinos have their own racial issues in this country, but Native Americans and Black people have been dealing with it the longest.

I have learned to be lonely through employment, legalized segregation, church, meetups, college, so-called family reunions, and other aspects of my life. It's not like I can rewind the clock and go back to high school like Drew Barrymore in Never Been Kissed....NO! This is real life with real problems, and I feel like I am in the eye of a tornado just waiting for it to drop me on the ground. See, the resources that I keep somehow accumulating will run out and I will find myself without options. Section 8 only allows you to stay on Section 8 if your rent and utilities are paid and even one of them gets terminated, then so are you from your housing, no matter how hard you try.

...and I just feel lost and claustrophobic in this whirlwind of a life, struggling to breathe and to survive. I don't want to be lonely, but it's not really my choice because not being lonely requires more than just one person. I can't wait until the affordable robotic companions. I have learned that not being lonely requires computer and technology connections, not human ones.

I tried pressing rape charges against my youngest child's father for what he did to me. I didn't do it until after 8 years, but it didn't matter because I had to go through the whole process all on my own. No one cared about me when it happened, and no one really cared when I was going through it. My youngest child's grandmother on her father's side blew smoke in my face when I was pregnant with my daughter after I had told her what her son did to me. She called me a whore. The hardest thing to do is to have no support when you go through something. The father and his family don't care about the nightmares that I have. They don't care about anything but themselves. When you are raped, it's hard enough dealing with the trauma, but when you are raped and alone, it's even worse. People call me stupid and ignorant and naïve, and that maybe so. To really be there for someone sometimes means just listening and having sympathy. Because of him, I forbid any male testosterone into my apartment. No one understands how traumatic it is to have such emptiness in a world full of such chaos than a person who has been raped. See, women are receivers, and men think with nothing but their penises. They don't care who they hurt or who they give their seed to as long as they're satisfied...but they are never satisfied. Their thirst for control and power is the ultimate thing that will eventually destroy them.

I remember my grandmother Heri a little bit. She loved me a lot. She made me feel loved, then she died. She was a church-going woman and I know that I would've loved her and being around her. We starred in a play together when I was younger, but the video quality of the recording is very low. If she had been alive, my life would've been different. I look at pastor's wives and their children and think that I could've been loved like that. I see how they treat each other. There are some children who don't like the being preacher's kids and having overprotective parents. I wish I had only had a father who loved me like some pastors love their children. Father daughter dances, birthday parties, conventions, anniversaries, and holidays are all events that should be cherished, but are also events that make me depressed. I miss my grandmother very much and I think about the events and situations that could have happened with her here. She was a very big family-oriented woman. You see the mothers in the church and the ambiance and presence they give when they are there, my grandmother was also one of those godly God-Fearing women. She would have taught me a lot. Sometimes, I feel left behind because I am never going to be able to learn about the things that only she could've taught me. People care about their own lives and their own families, not helping someone else catch up to where they should or should not be.

I just sit in my apartment trying to come up with creative outside of the box ways of changing and manipulating my situation for the better. It is very difficult, and I know that in the end, I always hit these roadblocks. My counselor kept telling me that I keep getting back up and then I thought, 'why do I keep getting back up just to keep getting knocked down again'. The feeling of loneliness is very hard to deal with especially when you have tried to fit in repeatedly, but you have yet to succeed. Too busy, not a part of their personal family, not a part of the clique in church, being different, not part of a sorority, different backgrounds, not a part of the in-crowd at church, just being the outsider are all reasons why computer technology friends and pets are better than human ones. I can't wait until the technology in the TV show *Reverie* comes out. I thought about it and I would be the first one to try it. The idea of the antisocial Americans always surrounded by technology will eventually make that kind of VR technology possible and better than the show. No one communicates without technology hardly anymore. The sad reality is, that someday, no one will probably have any human friends because we will all have computer ones.

Right now, there is a distinct possibility that I may have people who care about me. People who, in the event of an emergency, will drop everything to either help me or to find someone who can. Just because I have people who care about me, doesn't mean that I am not lonely. I don't have friends that I can talk to when I need to or hang out with me once a month. Loneliness is like darkness, empty and void and heavy. When I want to go somewhere, I have learned to go by myself....fill my emptiness with things and outings with myself.

I learned to be lonely because that's the way I have been taught by society majority of my life. I don't know if I will ever be whole again, but maybe I am better off being lonely than ever letting anyone ever hurt me again.

Sexual Abuse

Your penis is like a knife,
A knife that cut my heart.
You disrespected me,
You took my body,
I was your toy,
Your rag-doll.
I had no feelings,
I was not allowed to feel.
My breast were your bottles,
You cared not what I thought,
I was a child and I was wrong,
Everything was my fault.
I was made to like your touch,
I was made to want you.
But no matter what,
You made me throw up.
Your touch disgusted me,
Your face made me angry,
Your smell made me cry.
I hated you,
You took a huge piece,
Of what I was supposed to be.
You put me into degradation,
You cared not for my principles.
I couldn't grow up,
And catch up to where you were.
I couldn't be a woman,
And your twisted mind loved that.
You loved nothing but sickness,
That controlled your penis,
The one thing you used to think with.
How could you!
How could you tear my world apart,
How could you not love me the right way,
How could you treat me like a woman,
How could you become Satan's best friend,
When I was so small in every way!
I wanted to be accepted,
And you accepted me in the wrong way.

Now I am faced,
With a lifetime of pain,
A lifetime of healing,
A lifetime of feeling dirty and violated.
When men touch me,
I am sometimes not there,
I make myself numb,
So I don't re-experience what you did.
All who you are,
All who you want me to be,
As I look back and see all that I was to you,
I think to myself,
How ugly you made me feel.
But then I sit back and I pray to God,
That someday I'd be healed.
Someday, I'd be a shoulder,
For when you make someone else feel that way,
I'd be there for them,
I'd be able to tell them,
That God loves them,
And not in the sick, twisted way that you did.
I'd be able to tell them,
God will make everything new again,
And no matter what happened,
That God has never left their side.
And though it may be hard to trust again,
God is someone that they can always count on.

God has always been my father,
And God will always be,
A healer, guider, and protector,
Of my soul, spirit, mind, and body...
Thank You Daddy!!!

My Body Is Not My Own

An innocent young girl is so excited about her room. Her room is pink. Not just any pink, but cotton candy pink. She got to choose the color of her room and have it painted. She was able to choose any color she wanted, and she chose pink. The fumes to her new beautiful pink room were too strong for her to sleep in right now, but she wanted to anyway... but momma wouldn't let her, so she had to sleep in the dull, boring old living room with walls that were white. Not snowy white, just dull boring, crusty old white. As upset as she was, she was still so very excited. She laid down on the itchy, but soft couch thinking about her newly painted and very pink room. At least she had her favorite reddish orange blanket. It was made of cotton...not wool like cotton, but a nice soft cotton. She sucked on her blanket. It tasted really good. It was a very bad habit that she had never been able to get over. It made her feel comfortable. At least she didn't suck her thumb. She couldn't even remember falling asleep.

She could feel something on her forehead. It was a hand. She opened her eyes. Her head was on the painter's lap and he was brushing her forehead. Should she scream. Suddenly visions of what happened on some of her favorite TV shows flooded her head. She saw adults with grown men who screamed, and their throats slashed. She saw adults stabbed in the chest. She saw adults being beaten to death because they fought back. She remained quiet. The painter took the young girl into the bathroom, closed the door, and turned on the shower. "Put your mouth on it", he said motioning the young girl to suck his penis. She could feel his hand maneuvering her head up and down as she began to gag and felt like she would throw up. The man began moaning as he moved the young girl's head faster. Gagging, she didn't know what to do. She wished she had a dad and imagined that he would come in and catch her with this man's penis in her mouth. It just saddened her that no Daddy would ever love her that way.

The painter pulled his penis out of the young girl's mouth. The painter laid the young girl down flat on the bathroom rugs. The young girl could feel the penis between her legs. As the painter started moving on top of her, she imagined she was in her cotton candy pink room in front of her mirror. She had watched this one episode of Beyond Reality with Shari Belafonte, her favorite afterschool show. In this episode, this woman was able to go inside of a mirror. The young girl loved that episode. So, in front of her mirror, she began to put her hand out and proceeded through the mirror. On the other side of her mirror, was the same room, but with a brand-new bedroom set. She started to walk out the bedroom when she heard the painter moaning. She was suddenly back into the bathroom as the painter pulled his penis out of her and fluid began flowing from his penis onto her favorite blanket. The young girl just lay there, first looking at the painter, then at the blanket. The sad part was, this wasn't the first time a man had touched her.

Throughout my life, there have been many men who have touched, prodded, fondled, groped, kissed, and had sex with me in many different ways. I learned how to suck my first penis at the age of 9. As far as I can remember, I was first touched at the age of 6. The doctors have no idea when my virginity was taken. I can even remember the names of some of my abusers, but I will not mention them here. I became every man's toy, play thing, and sex doll. I had babysitters whose sons sexually molested me, babysitters who have allowed other boys to do it, my biological mother's friends who have come into the house and have touched and kissed me, and even men who just take pleasure in my body as a whole period.

There was a man at a high school, a janitor to be exact, who loved being inside of me. I was a newspaper carrier delivering him a newspaper and he was interested in more than just the paper. As he lay on top of me in one of the back rooms of the library, I remember telling him to please hurry because my biological mother would be looking for me and send the police after me. I knew that wasn't true though. His response was 'five more minutes'. The truth was that no one cared about what I wanted or felt when it came to my body and I soon learned that my body is not my own and did not belong to me. Men owned my body and they took pleasure in it whenever they pleased.

By the age of 13, I was in social services custody and still being touched by grown men. I was placed in a foster home temporarily. The lady belonged to a church that I went to. She had a fiancé. That fiancé used to touch my breasts and stick his hands down my pants a lot. His fingers would always go up and inside of me. I would always try and focus on something else to get my mind off of what was happening to me. The truth is, I always snitched after a man did something to me. Unfortunately, every time I snitched, some adult got mad over something about what I said or how I said it. I didn't tell them soon enough, why didn't I scream, etc. I just wanted men to stop touching me. This church lady though, she called social services and told them that I was a liar. Between she and social services, I was then labeled as **Jail Bait**. According to them, it was all my fault why men were touching me. That was the last foster home that I remember going to. There were more men after that. On staff member like rubbing on my legs. I was in a behavioral health center at that time. Boys and girls jumped me after I told on him. Apparently, that staff man was really popular.

At the age of 18, after I had been in their custody for over 5 years, social services emancipated me on the streets, homeless and pregnant by a convicted sexual offender. But let me back up a little bit. Social Services tried to place me back with my biological maternal parent. I met this man on a telephone chat line. When my biological mother chose her girlfriend (mate) over me and kicked me out, I became homeless and back on the streets. This man made a deal with me…. that he would give me a roof over my head in exchange for sex. So, I agreed to get off of the streets. I was young and naïve and soon found out that an agreement was just that, an agreement. I moved into his place and realized that I would forever be his sex toy. He had enough pornos to open up his own shop. They filled his closet and aligned some parts of his bedroom. This agreement was harder than I thought for me. I had to watch his pornos just to be able to get into him. After about a couple of months, I found out from a doctor that I was pregnant…. which was a shock to me because I had doctors who told me that I wasn't able to get pregnant due to all of the sexual abuse that I had. I had found out later in life, that I actually had a tilted uterus, so it wasn't impossible for me to get pregnant, it was just harder. This man also had many girlfriends who stopped by and one in particular hated the fact that he told her that I was better at oral sex than she was. She wrote 'fuck you' on the door, which got him kicked out. I was pregnant and homeless and slept on the streets from my third month to my sixth month.

When I got pregnant with my second child, it was by a man who raped me in a motel room that I had. I didn't have enough money to get an apartment, so I had a motel room that I paid for on a regular basis. I met him at a bus stop. He gave me his number and I gave him mine. When he finally called me, it was a few weeks later. He called early in the afternoon around 12pm or so and asked if he could come over. I was stupid (some people say naïve, but I say stupid) and said yes. He didn't show up until I was already prepared for and heading to bed. I was turning out the lights in the living room area when I heard this knock at the door. I looked out of my peep hole and say him standing there. I let him in and started fussing at him. He claimed that he had to catch the bus. This man had more than enough time to catch the bus. I told him that he needed to call somebody to come and get him. He picked up the phone and dialed a number. When he got off of the phone, he said his sister said she wasn't coming to get him, so I told him to leave. It was around midnight, I think. He said he didn't have any place to go so I told him he could sleep on the couch. This Budget Suites motel room had a bedroom, kitchen area, bathroom, and a living room space, but no doors on any of it. He crawled in my bed in the middle of the night and raped me. This whole ordeal is why no male species (even if you identify as a different gender) is allowed into my living quarters... not even my daughter's friends. I tell her to tell the exactly as I have said... no male species allowed in my house, period....no discussion. I called the police because this man cursed me out a lot when I told him to leave. "Man, you better go ahead with that shit!" The police came and escorted him outside. He was so high, he didn't even know his own name, so police had to go into his pocket and pull out his ID card. It wasn't until later that I found out he went by multiple aliases.

When I did find out that I was pregnant, again shocked, I tried to do the right thing. I tried to make things work out because I know what it's like to not know where you come from and my oldest daughter's father got to raise her. So, I wanted my youngest child to make her own decision about her father. I used a payday loan to get an apartment. This man raped me several more times when I was pregnant, showed up extremely drunk to meetings that I was trying to have with him...the times he showed up at all, and almost got me kicked out of my apartment. There was a taxi driver who called me telling me that this man was trying to get to my apartment but was too drunk to remember the address. I informed this taxi driver to never bring this man anywhere near me ever again. I left the state and went far away from him. I had had enough.

It became very depressing having men just use my body for whatever they wanted. When I got older than that, I was forced into prostitution by my own biological maternal parent. Men of all different races, sizes, and body types used my body for whatever they wanted and paid me for it. While the money was wonderful, I wanted something more. I thought that I could have something more. Little did I know that no real man would want something that was **damaged**. My body had not been my own.

My stepdad once told me while I was talking to him on the phone, that I was just like my biological maternal parent, a slut....in so many words. I had wanted to know at the time why he didn't protect me, and his response was, again in so many words, that I wasn't his child. I found that part out later in life, that I was just an agreement between him and my biological maternal parent. He wanted to marry her, and she told him that he had to adopt me first. So not only did social services believe that everything was my fault, but so did the only father I had ever known that was on my birth certificate.

When I am around men, I get very nervous, anxious, and uneasy. I have two sides to me though. See every man who has been inside of me, whether from sexual abuse, rape, prostitution, etc. has taught me how to please them. I have grown more confident over the years and by the time I was prostituting, perfected the art of pleasing men. While I do not like it, I have been learning about how to please men since I was 6 years old. Kama Sutra became my favorite thing to study and watch. I had never had any real father figures, older uncles, older brothers around. No, men in my life just wanted to sleep with me. It is a circumstance that will forever leave a whole in my heart. I know that some people say that being broken is a choice…that you have to forgive and forget…that God will heal everything if you ask Him…that it is a choice to let the past continue to hurt you, but when you have had as many men inside you as I have, the pain never goes away. I just wanted to be loved as a little girl. I just want to be loved by a man as an adult, not as a sex object of what I can do for him, but really loved by a man. I feel the pain when I am near men. The only way I don't, is to always be in control…and even then, I will feel it later.

It is even worse when people, especially church people tell you that you are choosing to stay in your current circumstance. I joined lots of sexual abuse support groups wanting to know how they fully healed from the pain, and pretty much all of them said that it is a lifetime healing process. One church lady told me that she doesn't even believe that I was sexually abused as much as I have said. It is depressing being a woman ripped open by men. I have "dirty" issues now. Every time, I am in or near water, I spit. I can still taste the sliminess of the cum in my mouth. I can't eat anything slimy at all. It makes me sick to my stomach. I use a lot of dish soap because everything has to be clean. I was up at least 5 times in one shower just to be fully clean. I always need my clothes to be really clean, so I use a lot of laundry soap and put the washer on extra rinse. I also use a lot of bathroom tissue to get clean…I have to constantly flush because I tend to stop up the toilet a lot. It is hard, very hard. Everyone wants you to get over it, like it is just a minor scratch on your outer skin that will eventually heal over time and be barely noticeable. A whole lot of stuff in our society is surrounded by sex. No one even stops and cares just how much all of that sex affects other people, so I don't say anything. I stop talking because everyone wants me to shut up. No one cares and so I put a **muzzle** over my mouth, keep everything in and suffer in silence. I dream about being married one day, but only in my alternate universe because I know that fairy tales are just for kids, and I became an adult a very long time ago, even before I was ever ready.

I tried pressing rape charges against my youngest child's father for what he did to me. I didn't do it until after 8 years, but it didn't matter because I had to go through the whole process all on my own. No one cared about me when it happened, and no one really cared when I was going through it. My youngest child's grandmother on her father's side blew smoke in my face when I was pregnant with my daughter after I had told her what her son did to me. She called me a whore. The hardest thing to do is to have no support when you go through something. The father and his family don't care about the nightmares that I have. They don't care about anything but themselves. When you are raped, it's hard enough dealing with the trauma, but when you are raped and alone, it's even worse. People call me stupid and ignorant and naïve, and that maybe so. To really be there for someone sometimes means just listening and having sympathy. Because of him, I forbid any male testosterone into my apartment. No one understands how traumatic it is to have such emptiness in a world full of such chaos than a person who has been raped. See, women are receivers, and men think with nothing but their penises. They don't care who they hurt or who they give their seed to as long as they're satisfied...but they are never satisfied. Their thirst for control and power is the ultimate thing that will eventually destroy them.

They say that if you have a problem, then you should pray about it. If you are raped, you should tell someone and report it to the police. There is power in the name of Jesus. When I tell someone, people ask me what I did to turn that person on? How did I give that person false messages? What did I do to make that person rape me? If I tell the cops, the look at me like I deserved it. The white man with the badge whose ancestors used to legally rape black women every day, now it's a crime. The white man with the badge who used to shoot the black man for sleeping with his wife when the wife used to force the black man to sleep with her. Black women are considered to be the scum of the world. Some races sleep with white people just to lighten up their own. A lot of black men won't even touch the black woman. So now, here I am a black woman stating that I have been raped. Not once, or twice, or even three times, but more than that. Why couldn't my Daddy have stopped men from raping me after three men, or four men, or even five? Why did I have to be sexually molested and raped so many times? Why do a lot of men get to get away with raping and abusing women? America put a man in office who abuses women and says discriminatory things out of his mouth and yet the biggest question I have is...what does that say about America as a whole? My Body As An African American Woman Is Not My Own And Does Not Belong To Me!??!

Indestructible Darkness

Shame is a very painful emotion caused by consciousness of guilt, shortcoming, or impropriety. Have you ever felt the dark, vast deepness of shame? It is a feeling that grows like an indestructible vine or weed. Shame will make a person want to crawl up inside of themselves and die. Shame makes people judge themselves as weak, and they tend to try and stay under the radar about what they are not doing because when the tasks of life go undone the risk of being judged by others constantly comes up. Even when the littlest accomplishment or task is completed, the smallest degree of satisfaction can be ephemeral. When you are feeling depressed or shameful, your brain does not give enough attention to positive experiences, and that bias toward noticing negatives mires people in the muck of depression and shame. Escaping this type of negativity is like trying to escape quicksand. By not noticing or remembering positives, future motivation, ambitions, and enthusiasms are impaired. If you cannot recall how good it felt to get something done, then the missing sense of accomplishment impairs your motivation, ambition, drive, and enthusiasm to act when feeling depression or shame's downward pull. Now, this behavior of not wanting to act becomes a shameful secret.

Strong feelings of shame stimulate the nervous system, causing a fight-flight-freeze reaction. We feel exposed all the time and want to hide or react with rage, self-loathing, and darkness, while feeling exceedingly alienated from others and the good parts of ourselves. We may not be able to think or talk clearly to ourselves or others and the feelings of self-loathing is made worse because we're unable to be rid of ourselves. This can also make it hard to ask for help from others. Facing them, approaching them, talking to them, and/or even trying to seek affection from them can cause even more shame.

I started writing this book in my 30's. Between the ages of 13 and 18, I was a in the custody of the state. While in social services custody, I didn't go to school like other kids. I was handed a book and asked to complete work from it. Whether my answers were right or wrong, I was given an A. I know what my transcripts looked like because the very first community college that I went to showed them to me. I had a 4.0. How could I have gotten a 4.0 if I had never really been to public high school before. After being inside of locked facilities for five years, I was released on the streets homeless and pregnant by a convicted sexual offender. I had no idea what to do and didn't even know how to live in society. The feeling of living on the streets from three to six months pregnant was shameful and depressing enough, but my shame started long before that.

My very first college degree was an Associate of Applied Science degree. I majored in Multimedia. School was always a struggle and was another huge shameful part for me. I always had to fight harder than everyone else to prove myself. It took me 6 community colleges, about 4 states, and 15 years to complete my degree. It was the only thing I consistently focused on once I got out of the system. I have no idea who put the idea in my head to go to college, but I did. Once I graduated, everyone else was a lot happier than I was. I did accomplish getting my degree, but it wasn't an accomplishment that I was greatly proud of.

I had been trying to get jobs almost the entire time that I was released in order to take care of my children. No one cared what I went through, they just wanted to hire someone who wasn't me. Then on top of all of that, being in the great northwest and all of its systemic racism didn't make things any better. I tried doing whatever I could to feed my children and keep a roof over their heads. Every job that I have ever had felt like a defeat. On the east coast, I got hired, but only part-time. While going to school, working two part-time jobs, and trying to be a single mother, I had really no help. Childcare was at least $250/week and bills were more than I could handle. I essentially moved over to the great northwest in order to get help from my biological mother with childcare.

Going to school in the beginning was difficult because I had to pick a profession that would help me take care of my bills. I tried emergency medical technician, then elementary education, and then general studies. I fell short on all accounts. Remembering vocabulary and terminology was extremely difficult and I kept failing every single class. On top of that I had never taken SAT's, or ACT's before. I needed a degree in something that I was good at…something in which I wouldn't constantly fail every single class. One community college told me that I was not even on college level and that the government had set me up for failure. One of the counselors and teachers tried to get other teachers to pass me so that I could get a degree and go to work, but not all of the teachers agreed. By the time I was at my sixth community college, I had 2 high school diplomas and a GED.

Getting my degree only felt like more of a defeat. Number one, getting my degree didn't help me to get a great job. I tried being a Digital CTE Teacher teaching multimedia to kids and found out that I needed a digital cte certification. I tried researching it and came up short. I also tried applying for a lot of other jobs as well. Even though I had the experience and the portfolio to back it up, most jobs required a bachelor's degree. I even had an employment specialist helping me.

While I have sought out counseling, it is easier for me to write than to talk. When I try to make friends, I always come up short. People have told me that they have friends from way back in high school. I have also been told that high school is the foundation for communication. I had one counselor who told me to pay for eHarmony for a year and try to learn how to communicate that way. It didn't really work. So, what about me? No one tells me what I am doing wrong in terms of trying to make friends. Having no friends is also very depressing. People make a lot of excuses why they don't want to hang around me and I get it. So, I stopped asking I stopped trying to talk to them. I internalized my emotions as much as I could. I listened to headphones, so I wouldn't have to talk. I go to church and even they don't get it. You see people once a week and we're supposed to be family. To me, it feels like a strip tease, you can look but don't touch or get too close.

I haven't yet figured out how to deal with my shame. People say that if you change your attitude, then you will change your circumstances, but the truth is, that's not true. I know how to fake it until I make it, but faking it is tiring. I am worn out by pretending like everything is okay. If I want to talk to someone, they pretend to listen. I know because of the way they respond to me. I listen and I am like, did you not hear what I just said, or did you just ignore what I said altogether. No one really understands how shame can break someone and I don't think really anyone cares. We all have our own baggage. I remember Bishop T.D. Jakes saying one time that sometimes people don't want to be around someone because they are too heavy. Maybe that's how people feel about me.

My shame comes from many different circumstances in my life. Revelation 9:6 says: in those days people will seek death but will not find it. They will long to die, but death will flee from them! I remember in social services custody how I tried killing myself a lot of times. I took a whole bottle of sleeping pills…nothing happened. I opened my vain a lot and tried to drain my blood. One time I filled to sheets full of blood. The staff member came in smashed my face in my blood, dragged me down the hall by my hair and threw me into time out. I tried digging all the way down in the crease of my arm where nurses usually take your blood. I was determined to cut the vein, but I couldn't find it. To this day, nurses can't find it either. I can only have blood drawn on the right arm now.

Shame can feel overwhelming. Shame can feel increasingly dark. Shame can make you feel intense stage fright when there is no performance. Shame can make you feel claustrophobic. Shame can make you depressed, sad, and lonely. Shame can keep you up all night. Shame can drain everything in you. Shame can make you feel exhausted. Shame can make you have high anxiety. Shame can also be the death of you spiritually, physically, emotionally, and even sexually. The indestructible darkness that I feel every day can't be fixed by some stupid drugs. It can't be fixed by some radiation or laser treatment. My shame is real, and it hurts all the time. People don't understand and so I just stay quiet and watch the minutes go by.

Ecclesiastes 4:9-12 talks about how two is better than one and how three people together cannot easily be broken, but someone who falls alone is in real trouble. There are many scriptures in the Bible about love and how it can heal a broken heart, conquer all, never ends, and is more powerful than anything. Song of Solomon 8:6 states that love is as strong as death. 1 Corinthians 13 is a whole chapter on love about how to love. I know that my Father in Heaven loves me. Sometimes, I wish that a human being did to…of course not the way Jesus does. Maybe someday, somebody will truly love me for who I am and without stipulations or limitations. Until then, I have to deal with my constant indestructible darkness.

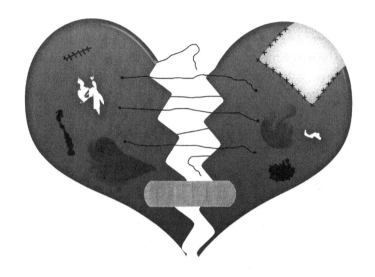

The Girl Without The Man

My Daddy means the world to me. He loves me beyond anything that I can ever imagine. When I was little, I used to spend a lot of time with Him. He would answer my questions whenever I asked Him. I was innocent and loved by Him. I was naïve and cared about Him more than life itself. I never wanted to grow up. I knew that no matter what happened, I would always have my Daddy. I would always be His little girl. I don't remember the first time I ever met my Father. I don't remember the very first time I ever got saved because for me, I have rededicated myself and have gotten saved more than a million times. I have been baptized just as many times as I have been saved. There is one constant....my Father never changes, even though the feeling that I feel changes every time I am saved and baptized again.

Have you ever had a supernatural experience? Have you ever felt the presence of God? Have you ever felt the touch of Jesus? Like the woman in the movie Edward Scissorhands spinning around in the snow like she had done that for the very first time in her life. Like a burst of fresh air that you have never felt before. Like a healing breeze that flew from the mountains. Like a morning glory, you never realized was even there. Like a nice hot shower that never goes cold. Like a fresh drink of water that you have never tasted before. Like a soft cloud that you have never slept on before. Like soaring high above mountains and hills and plains. Like an inner peace and an extremely long sigh of relief. Like the most enormous, most comfortablest, most peaceful, most serene, warmest, happiest hug that you have never felt in your entire life....and probably will never feel by a human being. A supernatural experience with the presence of God is like that times infinity. I love my Father more than life itself. I don't want mansions, or riches, or gold, or anything but Him. I want to curl up in His lap and just bask in His glory. I want to just be with Him. I want Him to wrap His arms around me and never let me go. I need Him to hold me…just like He used to. I need Him to surround me with His presence. I love Him so much! I love Jesus! I love God. I know that nothing can separate me from His love, even though that's not always how it feels. I need my Father more than anything. The presence of God in indescribable. It is a feeling that you will never forget, a feeling that once felt, will eat you alive, a feeling that you will long for because of the richness, the enormity, the fullness of it. I love my Father! I want nothing more than Him. I need my Daddy when I wake up and when I go to bed. I need my Father everywhere I go. I love Him so much!

Lęwa Ubunifu

I imagine my Father holding me in His arms. I, curled up like a little baby, and Him holding me ever so softly looking down at me. I can never forget the love that my Father has for me…the love that He has always had for me. He knew me before I even entered my biological maternal parent's womb. He wrapped me in His arms and kissed my forehead ever so softly. The love of my Father is one of pure love, love that is perfect and whole, not broken and corrupt. I will love my Father forever and ever for all eternity. Even when I make mistakes, My Daddy will always be my Dad. I know that He will always love me. I just remember Him always being there for me until the day I betrayed Him. The day that I listened to humans over Him. That was the day that I felt numb and my feelings seemed to die hard. That was the day that I looked this woman in the eye and asked her if she would ever lie to me and instead of trusting my Father, I trusted her. I was stupid, naïve, and dumb that day. That was the day, I lost everything…including myself.

My Father has done a lot for me. Sometimes, I have to stop and really look at all of the great and wonderful things that my Father has done for me because I forget. He helped me to graduate college with my Associate's Degree. It took me 15 years, 5 community colleges, and 4 states later to complete that degree. He wrapped his arms around me every time I was sad, lonely, and depressed. Yes, he has forced me to grow up, but He also took me from the dark places when it got too rough. He has carried me through the thickest of woods. Even when I want to turn and cave in and give up, he surrounded me with people that do not give up on me. He kept me alive for over 18 years after I got out of social services custody. He has been healing me, not always the way I want him to, but the way I need to be. He brought forth out of me 2 beautiful and healthy baby girls. He allowed me to travel for 10 years and see the beauty that the United States has to offer. I have traveled and been through Mount Monarch, Oklahoma, Dallas Zoo, Walt Disney World, Washington, Kings Dominion, Oregon, Busch Gardens, California, Universal Studios, Texas, Ohio, Enchanted Forest, Utah, Give The Kids The World, Maryland, VA Beach, Florida, Louisiana, Oregon Story Board, Germany, Comedy Sportz, and New Mexico. I have been on the radio and have had my own TV show on a local TV station. I have also appeared on another local TV show called the Poet Heads. I have been homeless, but even when I was, my Father had people taking care of me. They would come and give me food, they brought me blankets, and my Father has protected me from getting raped on the streets and being addicted to drugs and alcohol. I thank my Father for the technology that I have. I have a PC, a mac, Google Cardboard, two iPod Shuffles, Samsung VR, and an iPad. I have a roof over my head, and I am not worried about where my next meal is going to come from. I have my own car that works. I have been very blessed to have a Father who loves me so much that he died for me. I have a lot to thank my Father for.

The Holy Trinity consists of the Father, the Son, and the Holy Spirit. I have always called God my Father. I never really had a dad. I remember that I had a stepfather who claimed that he loved me. Then people started telling me that he wasn't my real father. He never tried to help me like he helped his own children. He pushed me away lots of times, but on my birth certificate he was. I later found out that I was just an agreement between the two of them…my biological mother and my stepfather.

My mom seems to think that all men are dogs. She says that all they ever want is sex and that they will never want anything else. My Daddy was different. When I was in social services' custody, he would hold me when I was suicidal. He was there for me in my youth. He warned me about the people that I had around me and my oldest daughter. He separated us. I looked one of those evil people in the eyes asking them if they would ever lie to me and they told me no, but the whole entire time, they were conniving and sneaking around behind my back. I soon learned that people who call themselves Christians do a lot of evil while they are in leadership and all in the name of God.

I have been to a lot of churches. I have been saved and baptized a lot of times. I have joined a lot of churches, and I have been kicked out of a lot of churches. I was told that church is all about fellowshipping with other Christians. The Bible calls us to do that, but I soon learned that it didn't mean what I thought it meant. I used to like going to church. I would hear God's word and see people that I thought cared about me. Then one day, I was placed in the custody of social services and I soon began learning the reality of the so-called 'church'.

I love Jesus very much. The Bible says that we shall know Him by his fruit. The fruits of the Spirit are: love, joy, peace, forbearance, kindness, goodness, faithfulness, gentleness, and self-control. The Bible also says to beware of wolves in sheep's clothing or false prophets. It is hard trying to distinguish who is and who isn't a false prophet or conniving when looking through natural human eyes.

I am not really sure how to get to know people very well, but I know that one pastor told me that my issues were on the outside while other people's issues are on the inside. He made it very clear that I was different and weird and not welcomed at his church. He also told me that the only reason why I had been raped and sexually abused so many times was because Satan put a mark on my forehead. I have actually been told a lot of things about myself from church people. One missionary told me that she didn't believe that I had been raped and sexually abused as many times as I have said. She told me that some of those were obviously my fault.

As a matter of fact, that same missionary told my youngest daughter, who was only eight at the time, to never speak to her one Sunday because she doesn't say hi to her every Sunday. This wasn't the first time that she had said this. This was a woman who never comes up to you and says hi on her own....no, you have to go to her. If you miss even one Sunday, she gets upset. I remember when I first went to that church. I didn't know anyone and she was the first one to bite my head off. She always made me feel bad about myself. It was only because of the Pastor's wife in which I stayed.

I hate churches. They make me feel uncomfortable and awkward. It's like a fashion contest every Sunday. It doesn't matter whether it's small churches or big churches, they are all the same. All I want is my Dad. I used to imagine that I was in this big beautiful garden. There was no one there but my Father and I. I would talk to Him about everything and He would talk back. I loved Him. He made me feel safe and protected and loved. I had no fear of Him, and I looked at Him like most loved children look at their Father. To me, He was the greatest Dad in the world. I would read the Bible like a child reading her father's book that he wrote just for her.

After about the sixth or seventh time (I don't really remember) that I was violated, my image of my Father began to change. When I saw Jesus, he had a penis. I tried to shake the image from my head, and it made me cry so bad every time I thought about it. I soon became not so innocent anymore. I still loved Him, but it was hard for me to close my eyes and pray.

When I innocently told one worship leader about how much I loved my Father, she made fun of me. I didn't want anyone but my Daddy. I didn't care about anything else. When I cried, I cried for Him. Then after more sexual abuse, the image of my Father became very tainted, especially once I got out of social services custody. So, I would pray with my eyes open. There were times however, when I would somehow forget about what gender my Daddy was. I wouldn't see Him as a man, I just saw Him and didn't even notice His gender.

I eventually stopped loving to read. Reading the Bible is one of the only ways to communicate with my Daddy, so I felt really bad about not spending enough time with Him. I have always wanted to make Him proud of me. I feel like I fall short all of the time. Recently, I have been faced with an important question. Jesus healed people, raised people from the dead, heals people today from all sorts of things, but why didn't he stop just one or two or three of the men from my past from raping and molesting me? Why was it so necessary for me to go through all of that sexual molestation and rape?

I loved my Daddy unconditionally and blindly. I just wanted Him to love me back. I wanted to make Him proud of me. I told a first lady that I didn't want to grow up and she said that not wanting to grow up was selfish because we do not get saved and heal for us but for others so that we could be there for other people who go through things that we have went through...but who will be there for me?

Missionaries and pastors and prophetesses have told me that I have to want to be healed, that I have to want to be saved. I know that I have tried receiving the Holy Ghost for years. They stand you in the front of the church and tell you to say 'thank you Jesus' over and over again and apparently something is supposed to happen. I remember being told to open my mouth and just let go. I also remember being told to just 'speak' and I used to think, speak what? I would get so upset at myself because I wasn't good enough. I would cry and cry and feel so bad. I wanted a supernatural experience. I didn't really care about other people as much as I wanted my Daddy, but it was always strange to me. I hated going to the front of the church too. My self-esteem every time I went to church just became lower and lower. You see people in the church in leadership who are mean to you and evil and they get the Holy Spirit, so why couldn't I? What was wrong with me? Why did my Daddy love them more than me?

I miss my Daddy. I miss Him very much. I miss Him, the way He was when I was a child. When you are young, things are better, you are innocent, but when you grow up, you get lost, screwed up, and no one cares about helping adults. Adults expect other adults to just know what they are supposed to do. Asking for help is a sign of weakness. I didn't want to grow up, but unfortunately, I did. I grew up a lot between 2014 – 2018. Now I just feel lost like a little child crying in the middle of very dense woods searching for her Father. I need my Daddy, but all I can feel is pain and hurt and loneliness. I am tired of going to churches. I just want my Daddy, no one else. I want Him to hold me. I don't want to continue being the girl without the man, the girl without her Dad. I need my Father to find me before it's too late.

"Be strong and courageous! Do not be afraid or discouraged. For the Lord your God is with you wherever you go."
~Joshua 1:9 NLT

Prologue

This poem, *My Very Last Thoughts Before I Committed Suicide*, is intended to be used solely and for the purpose of the intent to give voice to those who are depressed, suicidal, or have suicidal ideation. This poem is in no way a tool to help, assist, or aid, any individual to commit suicide, begin suicidal ideation, or deepen their depression. It is my advice that if you are an individual who feels any of the feelings in the following poem, to please seek help immediately either by someone you trust or by someone who is authorized to handle your specific situation. If you do feel that you are suicidal, have suicidal ideation, or are depressed, please contact the National Suicide Hotline listed below.

National Suicide Hotline – 1 (800) 273-TALK (8255)
National Hopeline Network – 1 (800) SUICIDE (784-2433)

My Very Last Thoughts
Before I Committed Suicide

Will you remember me,
If tomorrow I wasn't here?
Would you remember me,
If you never saw me again?
Would you remember me,
If every time you called I never answered?
Would you remember me,
If everyone told you I was dead?
If I died tomorrow,
What would you say?
If I committed suicide,
Would you still love me?
Better yet, have you ever loved me?
How many times have you told me you cared?
How many times have you taken the time to hold me?
How many times have you said, "I love you" to me?
How many times have you written me a note?
Am I really that bad of a person,
That you won't even say hi,
When you see me?
Am I really that bad of a person that every time we talk,
Everything is always my fault?
Am I really that bad of a person,
That every time you bump into me,
You always scowl at me?
Does anyone love me?
Does everyone hate me?
Does anyone care?
Why can't I ever do anything right?
Why am I such a bad person?
How come I can't keep friends?
I don't ever know what I am doing!
I don't ever know what's wrong with me!
I don't ever know how to fix the way I feel!
I tell the truth, but people always think I am lying,
Do you hate me that much,
That you would rather just put me on drugs than love me?
I just want the pain to stop!
I just want to be free!

Caged and Locked

The drugs aren't working,
The manipulation from others,
Keeps pulling me down.
The condemnation from leaders in my community,
Makes me feel worthless.
I just want to die!
I just want to die!
I just want to die!
Everyone thinks I can heal by myself,
Everyone thinks that prayer will solve everything.
Maybe God just doesn't love me,
Because my prayers are never answered.
No one will help me,
Because they say I have to help myself...
But it is myself who is depressed and hurting.
What am I supposed to do?
If I knew how to fix me,
Don't you think I would've been fixed by now?
Someone please help me!
Don't stop me from trying to die!
Help me die!
Some people want to live, but I,
I really want to die...

Why do you think that I succeeded in my goal:
JUST TO DIE!!!

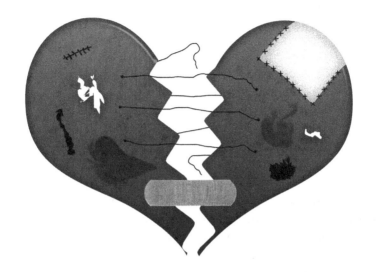

Prologue

This chapter, *The Bottomless Pit Broke My Fall,* is my personal experience with depression, suicide, and suicidal ideation. This chapter is in no way a tool to help, assist, or aid, any individual to commit suicide, begin suicidal ideation, or deepen their depression. It is my advice that if you are an individual who feels any of the feelings in the following chapter, to please seek help immediately either by someone you trust or by someone who is authorized to handle your specific situation.

If you do feel that you are suicidal, have suicidal ideation, or are depressed, please contact the National Suicide Hotline listed below.

National Suicide Hotline – 1 (800) 273-TALK (8255)
National Hopeline Network – 1 (800) SUICIDE (784-2433)

The Bottomless Pit
Broke My Fall

The bottomless pit broke my fall. I fell down and was jolted by the fact that I hit something. Though I could not understand what it was, I was hurt, cheated, and confused. This bottomless pit was supposed to be, well, bottomless. Instead I hit something, and it naturally shocked the hell out of me. I stood up trying to use my night vision but the darkness was so vast, I couldn't see a thing. How long had I fallen, I stand there and wonder. What will I do now? Will I have to stay down here forever or will someone rescue me? Am I able to rescue myself? How will I ever get out? Do I really want to get out? I feel around with my hands to feel the cold, dark, empty carcass. It's rough and... I cut my hand on something. I can feel the blood running down my hand as I can't help but realize that my situation has gotten worse. What will become of me and does anyone really care?

So many times, in my past have I gone through such emptiness and loneliness. So many times, have I asked myself these important questions of if anyone cares what happens to me. As a Christian, my main focus is supposed to be on Jesus and how He loves me. How can Jesus "fix" me because He is the only one who truly knows me? We should never take our eyes off of Him, for when we do, we begin to lose hope, faith, and sink like Peter did while walking on the water. It was only Jesus that brought him back to the surface telling him that he had very little faith.

As a person suffering from Circumstantial Depression, it gets hard to stay focused on Jesus. See I know what He can do. I have seen it. Miracles day after day, night after night. The question for me is not what He can do, but what *will* He do. *I look to the hills, from where does my help come from? My help comes from the Lord* (Psalm 121). So many times, I am faced with the question of what will my Father do. I get tired and weak and cry tears of pain and anguish....but I never completely die in the bottomless pit, even though sometimes it feels like I already have.

Suicide for me wasn't even a thought in the beginning. I didn't even really know what suicide was. I was raped by this janitor at a high school when I was in the fifth grade...I was delivering papers, long story. I had also just been raped by another man in my own house. Then yet another man was groping me at a different time in my house. I was wanted by many men. My biological mother handled the situations the best way that she knew how, but the problem was bigger than she could handle and eventually spiraled out of control.

Eventually, long story short, I was put into social services custody, where not only would I be groped, fingered, fondled, touched, stroked, and wanted by many more males and females, but I learned what suicide really was without really knowing what the word "suicide" really meant. Two things that's really important to note right here: one, I was labeled "jail bait" at the age of 13; two, in my family, almost every female for the past five generations has been sexually assaulted. While in social services custody, I was given the first weapon, a pen. Carter G Woodson once quoted, "A Pen Is Mightier Than The Sword". At the age of 13, I began writing poetry.

I felt so lost and alone. Everyone kept telling me that everything was my fault. My physical, sexual, emotional, and spiritual abuse was all about me and about how I needed to change my behaviors and ways. Churches blamed me, my biological mother blamed me, social services blamed me, and men blamed me. It was all me. I didn't want to live because no one cared about me anyway. However, I couldn't let others die. My heart was so full of love that I couldn't watch others die. When this girl and I decided to try and attempt strangling ourselves together, she turned blue and I didn't. I panicked for her and tried to save her. I never cared about me.

Over the course of five to six years in there, I became creative at trying to end my life. In the placements that I was in, I saw people who had jumped in front of trains and lost their limbs, people who shot themselves in the head and had the scars to prove it both physically and emotionally, people who had taken pills, people who had tried to drown themselves, and so many more people who had tried to commit suicide in all different ways and failed to succeed. I was determined to find a way that wouldn't allow my limbs to be taken or for my body to be left paralyzed just so I could forever be repeatedly raped.

I tried digging in my arm in the crease of my elbow so I could cut my vein. I dug such a big whole, but could even find the vein. To this day, neither can the doctors and nurses. I tried opening my vein in my hand where they draw my blood and after two or three sheets filled with blood, I didn't even pass out. I tried raising the dead, taking a whole bottle of sleeping pills, getting Satan to kill me, and cutting my wrist. No suicide success. I never got access to a gun except for once, but the idea that I wouldn't be successful at it, scared me. I wanted to do something that I knew for a fact would be 100% effective. So I tried to get more and more creative at trying to kill myself. I always tried to hide myself. My place to hide, my place of calmness, was the bathroom. No one really bothered me in the bathroom too much, that was until I got to a new church in the early 2000's.

Suicide, suicidal ideations, and just wanting to get rid of the pain, for me had always been on my mind. The feeling that no one cares about you is reprehensible. See, I felt for the longest time that people hate me, don't love me, and wouldn't care if I just mysteriously vanish or disappear. Some people love me only when they have power over me and try and control me, this is true, but then there are others who just won't leave me alone....and deep down inside, I guess I really don't want them too. I look in the mirror, now in my 30's and wonder to myself where I will be at, look like, or even feel like in my 40's. I wonder because where society says that I should be, is nowhere near where I am at. The physical pain I feel when I am sitting in the bathroom alone is excruciating. I think about everything negative that everyone has ever said about me...and it's been a lot. I think about kids who have parents that cuddle them at night, read to them, and love them with all of their hearts. Then I look at me.

I never want to hurt my biological maternal parent's feelings because she has her own shit to deal with and I will never understand her, but what I needed was for her to love me regardless of where I was, how much power she *didn't* have over me, and through how much pain I felt. Her mouth kept telling me that she was never going to change and to accept her as she was or leave her the hell alone, but she did end up changing a little bit. She changed slightly and I pushed more.

I wish that I could let things go and move one and just do what everyone wants me to. I wish I could forget everything that has constantly happened to me over the last 30 years. I wished that I could be free from the pain that I feel....but I don't know how, so I can't. No one will ever understand. Being in social services taught me a lot about how people will love you out of obligation. When you are in the system, there may be people who have to love you because you are a ward of the state and that's their job, but then there are other who couldn't care less about what their job is, and they choose to hate you because of their own selfish reasons.

One time, after I had filled two or three sheets full of blood, a person in charge came in my room, smashed my face in my blood, and dragged me down the hall while I fought the whole way. Another time, this same person allowed two girls to jump me while in a small corner bathroom. No one cared about that. To my biological maternal parent, I was the reason why I was in there....because I wasn't good enough. To the church, I wasn't their child, they didn't have to love me anymore, and I wasn't good enough. If I had really wanted my Daddy, if I had prayed more, love Him more, then He would've helped me, He would've set me free, but I didn't want Him enough. The church could never understand how much love I felt from my Dad. Despite what I was going through, He held me in His arms. I loved Him. He was the reason why I was never going to die in my adolescent and teen years, no matter what I did. I started hating my Dad. I told Him that I needed Him to let me go…just let me die. I didn't understand why He kept me around if I was so bad and couldn't do anything right. No one loved me and that how I had always seen the world. No one understood me and no one wanted to. Part of me is still stuck inside of social services custody and may never get out. That part of me is still lost and hurt and forgotten by everyone except for me.

Someone told me that the reason why I still feel the pain from my past is because I keep talking about it. They don't understand that when I shut up, I just feel worse. I don't really talk to anyone now except my counselor. With my Dad, I don't know what to say. I don't really know what to ask for. So, I stay in my corner and sometimes say nothing. As an adult, I know that when you talk about certain things, everyone wants to put you on drugs and lock you up. No one really wants to help you pull through it. In order to rise up from circumstantial depression, the circumstances have to change. Being drugged up is like putting someone in a medical coma for a cat scratch on their leg that swell up because the person's allergic to cats. The doctors hoping that the swelling will go down the longer they have that person induced. The problem is, that the swelling never goes down because a medical coma will not fix the problem. The problem is the cat scratch and if it is not dealt with, the medical coma will be the least of the doctors' worries and will become a problem in itself. However, no one wants to even look at the cat scratch let alone deal with it, and the medical coma becomes an epidemic. Soon the hospital is full of patients in comas with minor injuries that could have long been healed and rectified. The time the patients are in medical comas, however, is time that creates more problems and issues. Some of the patients have been abused. Some of them have been neglected. Some of their allergies to the scratch have gotten worse and have now spread throughout the body. Some of the scratches get better as the body becomes immune to that particular allergy…only for them to get another one, like stung by a bee, and then go back into a medical coma. Some of the patients miraculously just get better, come out of the coma and walk out of the hospital by themselves. Some patients get better but now need physical therapy. Some of the patients have died. The doctors never really deal with the scratch on most of the patients and in time, the patients just become statistics.

Belonging to a group can help with suicidal ideations or it can just make it worse. I developed codependency. I needed to learn how to "fish", but people just gave me "fish". So, I learned that I needed people to love me. However, I didn't want people controlling me. I needed them and their love, but when they were gone, I became depressed all over again because they didn't love me anymore. I then learned to deal with the emptiness, which is exactly how I felt when I was in social services custody. The bathroom was my haven, my place where no one bothered me. If I was in public, I went into the handicapped stall. If I was in a church, I tried to find a bathroom that most people didn't go into. The blackness, the darkness, the emptiness became a nuisance and wouldn't go away. I got used to it and learned to tolerate it. Years passed and people came and went and I got stuck and have yet to get out.

No one really bothered me in the bathroom too much, that was until I got to a new church in the early 2000's. This church was different. I told them to go to another bathroom, I was using this one. I said I was taking a dump, but they wouldn't leave. It confused me. There were two bathrooms in this church and this happened to be the smallest one. I told them to go into the men's bathroom. They left, but then came back. They were a nuisance. They kept asking me if I was okay. I told them I was fine, leave me alone. I was using the bathroom. The truth was that I was really upset. I was falling again. Somehow, I had managed to get up in the darkness about 30 feet but I couldn't see the top that well. Now I was falling again. These people didn't understand the rules. I go into the bathroom, you leave me alone. Forget about me. Every five or ten minutes, they came back. Then silence. Okay, now I could finish crying in peace, silently, not to make a sound, clenching my teeth, and straining like I was being electrocuted. Then they sent HER in. This is a woman who has touched my life differently. She always prays over you....I can never understand how because I don't even know how to pray over myself let alone someone else. She always has the right words to say. She says She always asks God to lead Her before She goes into a situation. She has a lot of charisma. She is always very humble. She can calm the scariest of kittens out of a tree. She is completely bible-lead. She is gentle, wise, smart, and extremely nice. Why would they send Her in? These people didn't follow the rules, they played dirty. They sent in....the First Lady! She asked me if I was okay, I told Her I was fine. Then She said, "okay I will leave you alone, but if you don't come out in ten minutes, I am going to come back in and you can tell me what's really going on, Amen". I sat there thinking to myself, like, *she's not really coming back.* I continued to cry. I didn't know what I wanted hardly at all, but I just wanted the pain to stop. So depressing is the moment you realize that you really have no one in the world who loves you or cares that you exist. So confusing is the moment you also realize that loves manifests in many ways. I wanted to die that day, but I couldn't because I had an obligation…my youngest daughter. I would never leave her unless I was 150% sure she would be okay when I was gone. At that moment, I wasn't sure, so I knew I wasn't going anywhere, but the pain was still there. First Lady is really busy all the time, so when She came back, I told Her, She didn't have to. I would be okay. I knew how busy She was and I didn't want Her wasting time on me. I told Her part of my problem, the easiest part to fix. I knew She didn't have time to hear all of it. She was so loving and warm-hearted, and Her love filled my spirit and soul. A true First Lady gives love straight from God, not herself. The love is different, feels different, and reacts differently.

The problem is that when you meet a woman like First Lady, you will never be the same again. When you meet a person like First Lady and have circumstantial depression, you will always have that feeling in your gut that reminds you that She will never be your biological maternal parent. She will never teach you everything that you need to know. She will never guide you to where you need to be. She will never be able to give you what you need. She will never be your family. You will always be an outsider to Her. You will always come last in regards to Her children and Her family. She will only care about you while you are a member of the church. She will never care about you beyond the scope of what Her duty is in the church. Her elders and deacons sat me down and informed me of the hierarchy of the church and reminded me that she is just doing her job. The Bishop and First Lady have a lot that they need to do, so continually going to them was selfish and disrespectful to the church. She, now busier than ever, will always be a First Lady, and I will always be just another member of the church slowly drifting away and losing touch with reality. What did I really need from my Daddy? I needed Him to be my Father or just let me go. The idea that everyone loves you because of an obligation is depressing. She loves me because God told Her to. People of the church love you because Jesus commanded it…but what if He never did, would they still love you? That question doesn't matter because we are only supposed to rely on God, not man. So why be around man in the first place? Why bother? Because Jesus commanded us to fellowship with one another.

For me fellowship is very empty. I would rather just stay home and talk to my Dad, watch TV, or play my video games that I get paid to play. I never understood fellowship. You go to church, see people, say hi, hear the message, sometimes eat with them, then go home to an empty place. Then repeat everything the next Sunday. I don't have friends or family that I hang out with...it's just me...and my daughter.

The bottomless pit is cold, dark, and lonely. Everyone has their big solutions on how you get out. Do they really work? Not really. The only one who can take you out is...

So now what? I have this push and pull on my heart that I sometimes try to ignore. I try to ignore it because it hurts. I don't know how to just forget the past like my biological mother and some other church people say. Every day, I am knocked in the face by my past, when I apply for jobs, when I go to work, when I communicate with others, when I try to make friends, when I go to school, when I raise my daughter, when I go to church, and just living period. The idea that you can just forgive and forget, forget altogether, or just get over real trauma is ludicrous. I have tried doing workbooks, listening to meditations, hypnotizing myself, and more to try and stop the pain, but the truth is, the pain never goes away. You have to deal with it the best way you know how. I don't want to be drugged up and become a zombie or in a medical coma.....that stuff doesn't work. I don't want to be locked up. Right now, when I need to listen to my music and go for a walk, I have that freedom. It makes me feel good. When I want to go to church, my church, not some church that is picked for me, I have that freedom. When I want to eat dinner for breakfast, I can because I have a choice. When I want to go to Hometown Buffet and stuff my face instead of cooking, I can because that's my choice. When I want to go into my War Room and pray and cry, I can because I have that freedom. I may feel pain every day and every day may be a choice and a struggle for me to get up out of bed, but at least it's my choice...not a choice that is chosen for me. For me, telling people in the past that I had been suicidal was not a way for people to help me, but a way for me to get drugged and locked up. No one really helped you in social services custody. No one really wanted to know what you went through. They would write on their pads and stick it in your file. No one really cared how much you needed help, not drugs. You were worth gold to them. You being in their custody meant that someone got to bring home the bacon to their family while you lay in your bed having nightmares, flashbacks, and anxiety attacks about what you were and still are going through. When you are up in the middle of the night and can't sleep, people offer you sleeping pills and say talk to your therapist and go back to your room. No one cares and they still don't.

There have been a lot of times when I have gotten three of four hours of sleep per day and can't sleep. I wake up, make sure my daughter is okay, cover my daughter up, and write because I can't sleep and have no one I can talk to. I can't be selfish and wake someone up, so I write, and I cry. When I have nightmares, I can't run to someone and talk about it. Jesus already knows what I am going through and there are a lot of times, not all the time, when I do talk to Him. I definitely can't talk to my biological maternal parent. That's a conversation that just makes me feel worse, so I avoid it at all costs. When I have panic attacks, high anxiety, and dreams (whether good or bad) about what I am going through, I have learned to let it out, when I am able to, or calm myself down. I have to control me until I am no longer able, but for my youngest daughter's sake, I will always try. I will suffer in silence. She will never know...until she gets way older.

I have to remain in control. I am the adult. I am grown. I am a strong woman. The world we live in hates "weak" people. I have learned that people have their own shit, so don't put your crap on everyone else. That's why when we ask people how their doing, we are supposed to respond by saying blessed or fine. I am having to teach my daughter that. She tries to go into this long speech of how she's doing, and I try to explain to her that people don't really want to know how she feels, except for me and her counselor. It's a human custom, I guess.

She has nightmares sometimes, and I tell her to pray about it. I sleep on a dog pillow on the floor, you now one of those big ones from Costco. Ever since I had the epidural, it is difficult for me to sleep on a bed. A lot of times, it's hard for me to sleep on the floor. I think the pillow is starting to get flat....need to buy another one. My daughter though has a loft bed. A lot of times she can't sleep with me due to my sleeping arrangements. I need her to be well rested. I try to cuddle with her on the weekends though when I am not busy. The other factor would be that we are on Section 8 in an apartment on the third floor. The lady underneath us has no kids and told me that she was sensitive to noise. She complains about everything. SO, from 10pm to 7am (quiet time), we can't do anything. We can't take a shower, watch TV, or cook, or walk, or anything. We have to tip toe around our place and whisper if we talk. I make sure my daughter is in bed by 7:15pm, 7 days a week. I tell her the truth, we live in an apartment complex. She can't get up, period, until 7am. She gets in trouble for singing or making any kind of noise during quiet time. The landlord already issued us a 10-day notice for non-compliance for noise level.

I dream about the country. A place where I am free to grow my own food, run around, and make things from scratch. I have done woodworking before. I want to live in a house in which my daughter is free and the land is quiet with no neighbors. My daughter saw a video on TV at the dentist office where there was a house way out in the country. She said she wanted to live there because she gets to yell and stomp and bang. I just laughed.

The bottomless pit is sometimes cool. It is where your imagination grows and lives. Usually since you can't see, you dream. Disney encourages young girls to dream big. My daughter always remembers that saying and song from Disney, but then so do I. I try to dream of a better life for she and I…one where we no longer have to deal with people. One where we are just free to live off of a land and start our own history. Problem is, that isn't very realistic. For now, the bottomless pit is my home, but some day, I will reach the top and never look back.

Life Is Short

When I think about life
In all its glory
The people, the places
The things, the businesses
Entertainment and the morbid
I shudder a sigh of fear
And a small sigh of relief
Aaliyah, Left Eye,
Whitney Houston and Michael Jackson
All died at very young ages
It makes me sad to think
Life is just way too short
We sit in America
And try to build up our treasures
Everyone striving to reach
That good old American dream
The rich get richer
The poor striving mostly to survive
And a twenty-four-hour society
Beginning to crack and crumble
The dangers we must face
On an average and daily basis
Never amounting to the pieces
Of our small and fragile selves
That we continue to lose each day
Most just give away unknowingly
Every minute of every day
Every second of every minute
Time they don't know they need
The man who loves sex way too much
Catches AIDS at age thirty
The single mother on welfare
Suddenly finding a lump in her breast
Little girls playing freely in their yard
Kidnapped by a mere desperate stranger
The too much party animal
Dropping dead from an accidental overdose
The workaholic who just can't stop
Drops dead abruptly from a massive heart attack

The always on the go road-rager
Killed in an automobile accident
The man who harbored millions
Egotistical and self-centered
And thinks he is better than God
Unexpectedly sleep forever
Without a single clue why
We ignore the mere fact of time
And just how much of it we have left
Never knowing what day ours will end
We never stop and experience
The great stuff God gave us
The mountains, the plains
The beaches, or even natural structures
For preparing for the inevitable
Is much easier when you know
The exact time of your ruin
But the ignorance of that date
Lends carelessness everywhere
To even the smallest human being
But, no you are right
Do not pray to the God up above
Do not care about anyone else
Build up your riches and glory
Keep polluting this earth with violence
Keep going about your business
Keep striving to get off welfare not stopping to smell the roses
Keep drinking, gambling, and smoking
Keep hoarding, overeating, and stealing
And do not worry about the amount of sodium
And sugar in your everyday food
Because you are right
Nothing will ever happen to you
Keep ignoring the cries of the earth
Crazy tornadoes, hurricanes, and earthquakes
Keep ignoring the rumblings of the heavens
The clash and crack of Mother Earth
Keep pretending like you don't care
But tomorrow is not promised

Not even to you
But if you did die tomorrow
What legacy, name, or message
Would you leave here behind you
Where would your assets, if any,
Where would they all go
Was it really all worth it
Never to forget at even a second
Or a fraction of a sound
Just how short our tiny lives
Really, really are
Life Is Just Way Too Short

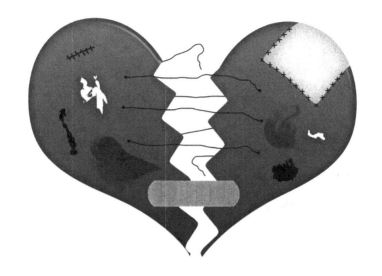

Grandma Heri Thamani
Wanyenyekevu

No one is perfect in any way
But I really loved my grandma
Who started out young
Learning solely how to raise
Her beautiful lovely children
Single and strong she was
She made a lot of mistakes
And even some of her children
Still held on to some of their anger
For the things she lacked
And the knowledge she finally gained
A little bit too late
When they were grown
And on their own
Then everything suddenly changed
And anger fled out the window
And for one very brief moment
Happiness filled the air
And some lives stood very still
A baby was born
On the fifteenth day of September
During her precious Auntie's
Own seventh birthday party
And grandma changed and became a new
And her heart became a pillow
And smiles the family possessed
On their faces back in eighty-two
And named right after grandma
Was beautiful baby girl, Heri
A precious jewel was she
With dimples like exactly like grandma
But no one knew about
The grandma way back then
Would never see this little girl grow
To be successful and independent
Or any adult age at all
Grandma loved that baby girl
Treated her with love and care
How precious that strong bond
That little baby had with grandma Heri
She played with grandma's wigs

And went to church on Sundays too
Sat right next to grandma Heri
Oh, how much I miss you
Your laugh, your smile, your style
The love you shared with me
Was gone too soon to last
I needed my only grandma
To show me how to love
But one fine day in ninety-two
Attacked she was they say
By the danger of the lumps
The pink ribbon that now stands
And the cure that came too late
Cannot erase the pain
For the trauma that baby would soon face
Losing her precious grandma
But never say goodbye
Someday I will see you again
And be united together
My wonderful grandma and me
And even though she never showed me
How to love her only God
I still know the quiet subtle hints
She still drops for me like crumbs of bread
O know my grandma still loves me
Teaching me just what to do
This little baby girl
Still feeling a little blue
And seeking her precious grandma
To come walking through her door
Wishing her to just come home
Never say goodbye
To the love and bountiful joy
Between my Grandma Heri Thamani Wanyenyekevu and me

**In Loving Memory of
My Blessed and Wonderful Maternal Grandmother
Heri Thamani Wanyenyekevu
December 2, 1944 - November 8, 1992**

Dahun Adura

My daughter,
My beautiful baby girl.
So silent, yet so awake,
So precious, and so well behaved.
Why does everyone covet you?
Why does everyone get so envious?
Your smile, your love, your cheerfulness,
Capture the hearts of so many.
Now thrust into social services' custody,
You look for me and long to be home.
In my arms you slept,
In my arms you cried,
In my arms you laughed.
Now being corrupted in a world,
Who looks at mothers with a close-minded heart,
Separating and severing our relationship.
Such a momma's baby you were,
So close you stayed beside me.
Now, only being able to look at my memories,
That I developed on paper,
And seeing you one hour a week.
I cry and cry longing to have you home again,
Sleeping right beside me.
Your four-year-old mind and creativity,
That continues to stretch and raise my creativity,
Is missed in my home of homes,
And my mind no longer growing.
My daughter,
My beautiful baby girl...
Always, remember that I love you so very, very much!!!

Teach Me How To Fish

Humans are conditioned to be the way that they are. No one starts from birth and says that they want to be lazy and a couch potato. Just like no one is in the womb of a woman and says that they hate a certain race because of the color of their skin or the way they talk or even where they are from. The sad reality is that humans don't need each other anymore and they have been conditioned to think that way. In slavery times, African American women were stripped of their name, hair, and heritage. In Africa, each tribe had different hair styles. Hair meant something to Africans. When slaves were brought to the US, their heads were shaved so that white people could have all of the slaves unified. They were then given white name. To this day, there seems to be more white and interracial couples than black ones. There are also all of these stereotypes about why black men choose not to date their own race. Black women are still looked down upon in the US for embracing their culture, natural hair, or for just being themselves. There are even certain countries and cultures today who literally tell people that they date the white race to lighten up their own.

There is an old saying that says, "If you give a poor man a fish, you will feed him for a day. If you teach him how to fish and you will give him an occupation that will feed him for a lifetime." This saying means so much in the United States today. The reality is that single parents have to work twice as hard in order to take care of their kids unless they have a profession that will pay a lot of money for their bills. ALERT: Not all single parents have had their children because they just naturally spread their legs willingly. The point is that back in the day, there were some parents who were able to teach their children "real" life skills: how to hunt, how to grow their own food, how to sew, how to cook, how to can, how to build their own house, and how to fix their car. The idea that Americans do not need to know these types of things today just puts them in a state of weakness. In the event of a major event, there would be a lot of Americans that would be lost. I thought it was interesting when I learned the amount of people going to Africa to help out…seeing as how Africa rejected the Africans America was trying to give back after slavery was abolished. The reason why it surprised me was because of the amount of homeless children we currently have in the United States. One celebrity stated that they didn't like helping out children here in America because they are too spoiled and selfish. That's funny when homeless kids barely have anything to eat. A pastor decided to help teens in Africa sew skirts and get them off the streets, but doing that for black kids here in America, I guess is too much.

The idea that we constantly look over seas to help out when children in America are dying left and right just seems really depressing to me.

I wish I had someone to teach me how to build my own house, can my own food, sew my own clothes, and grow my own food. Then I would really know how to take care of myself so much more. I see why the Amish life seems so enticing (outside of anything else that I didn't mention). Music and art and sports has been ripped away from our kids unless they can afford it. Everything these days, is about money and who has it and who can get more of it. Yeah, we don't need each other anymore which is why we will start killing each other more and more every day spiritually, emotionally, and physically if we are not careful.

A Child Saved... Is
A Soul Saved...

Church. What is the meaning of the word church. Technically the word means a building used for public Christian worship. Christian Worship is showing God the Father and His Son Jesus reverence and adoration. The Bible also talks about never neglecting to come together in fellowship. Fellowship is a group of people who have a connection or a link between them getting together for a purpose. I am writing this chapter solely based on my experience and knowledge and how it has affected me.

The "black" church was different in Africa and even in slavery times. After Africa, once "white America" took our culture, our tribal hairstyles, our clothes, our names, our humanity, the "church" with which we knew or even practiced was gone but not forgotten. Africans brought a lot of things to America from Africa including music, art, language, culture, folklore, and cooking/food styles. They also brought their own negro spirituals and stories with them.

The "church" back in slavery times didn't always represent a building. A lot of times, slaves got together whenever they could, especially underground. Negro spirituals and songs evolved during slavery from African culture to a means of survival and hope for the future. Faith grew into a beautiful artistic melody instead of the kind of faith that we mostly practice today. African slaves weren't given access to paper and pencil or copyright laws, so a lot of their instruments, music, stories, and art was stolen by their slave masters. Their slave masters felt that since they owned the slaves, anything that the slaves created belonged to them. Such stories as Anansi was adopted into America and ripped from African slaves and transformed into the Br'er Rabbit.

Throughout slavery, white slaves tried to monitor the so called "churches" in order to make sure that Africans were conspiring against them and to keep their slaves managed and in control, but churches among slaves just grew. It was the foundation for having a life of freedom, culture, and prosperity even though it may have been only through faith and inside those meetings.

After slavery, churches didn't stop meeting and the black negro church grew into public places fighting for cohesive African American communities. Black people got together at church in unison. They prayed, fed, clothed, and supported each other. They were "family". They didn't always see eye to eye, but they had each other's backs. It is important to note a couple of things right here. The Bible says in Genesis 11:1-9 (KJV): *"the people is one, and they have all one language; and this they begin to do: and now nothing will be restrained from them, which they have imagined to do."*

Also, the popular phrase "United We Stand, Divided We Fall" continues to ring out through America today.

Black churches were just that after slavery…a way to be united, but white oppression slowly began to take away from that. African American communities began to falter. The black church, in a lot of states, was no longer the pivot of our faith, community, drive, and determination. They slowly evolved and some disappeared.

Today, there may still be some black churches, but majority of them aren't as driven on creating cohesiveness in African American communities as they used to be. Some still celebrate and embrace African and African American culture, but most do not. The black church can be very confusing for a lot of people.

I have been kicked out of a lot of churches. I don't really fit in very well. I have been kicked out for getting pregnant out of wedlock, for *"my issues being on the outside and not on the inside"*, for being different, because of my depression and suicidal ideations, and because people hated me (anything they didn't consider to be normal). When I was in trouble and needed help, I ran to the church. I didn't know any better coming out of social services custody. Who taught me that the church was a safe place to run? I have no idea, but that's what I did….except, maybe I ran to the wrong church. At 19, I was very immature, but I always tried to tell the truth. I knew that the truth shall always set me free, so I tried to always tell the truth. People didn't like me. I was clingy, sociable, too friendly, and way too immature. Instead of someone trying to teach me, they rejected me. The worship leaders, the pastor and his wife, majority of the congregation….I was alone and instead of running away, I stayed. Why did I stay at a church that hated me? I don't know. I was young and stupid and I didn't know any better. In the end, I was the only one who lost out on everything. My home, my oldest daughter, my life. They took everything away from me and I hated churches.

I soon learned that all churches are not made equal. I wasn't interested in joining any more churches. I just wanted to have fun. I was invited to a Super Bowl party…at a church. How in the world do you have a Super Bowl Party at a church? OMG!!! It was so much fun. The First Lady told me that it's the same as in a home except, they don't drink and don't curse. I had one conversation with her and immediately became attached. Being codependent is hard because you don't know how to have your own self-worth without other people.

First Lady taught me a lot of stuff though....that was the biggest difference that I found with her from a lot of the other churches that I have been to. I could always ask her questions and she wouldn't get mad at me for asking them or hateful toward me because she thinks that I should already know the answer. There are quite a few times that I felt like she got frustrated with me because I didn't understand what she was either asking me or what she was telling me and I would keep asking questions for clarification purposes...but I don't actually remember the outcomes of those circumstances. I just remember telling her that I don't understand. First Lady showed me how to do things instead of always telling me. It's funny because I never knew you could mentally show someone anything, but she did.

The church today is not just comprised of just a First Lady. There is a Bishop, Deacons, Ministers, Pastors, Missionaries, Sisters, Brothers, Ushers, and Mothers. It can get quite confusing sometimes. For me, I have a hard time respecting authority in general, and especially if you are a man. I don't just do something because someone tells me to....at least not anymore. I question why you are asking me to do it. People in the church get mad at me because they are deacons and missionaries and expect me to do things because they said so....they ain't my parents. I always question why they are asking me to do it. Then I think about, *does it make sense to me why they are asking me to do it.* If it doesn't make sense, then I don't do it. A lot of them never understand why I just always did what Bishop and First Lady asked me, but never anyone else. That all comes down to who I am codependent on. The sad thing is, that reality has a way of slapping you in the face.

Watching people who I am codependent on, I realize that they may be a part of my world, but I will never be a part of theirs. I may share my feelings, hopes, and dreams with them, but they will never do that with me. I may want to invite them over my house, but they will never do that with me. If I have a problem, I share it with them, but they will never share their problems with me. I will invite them to my parties and other events, but they will never invite me anywhere.

So what have I learned by attending church....especially the black church in today's society. I have learned these things from attending and being kicked out of a lot of churches in general. I learned that I go to church on Sunday. I see everyone and then I go home. I learned that people at church don't really want to know how you are doing. If you don't currently feel a "happy" emotion, just say that you are "blessed". I learned that it is not up to people in the church to share in your highs and lows. Keep that to yourself and take it to God. I learned that everyone judges you at church when you don't look your best. The church is definitely a fashion show. I learned that the black church is not a general or African American community, but a "church" community. The main events that you will attend with "church" people is in the church. If you don't attend those events or go to church, then you probably won't see everyone. Outside of the church events, I learned that people's lives are private. There is a big DO NOT ENTER sign hanging on their personal space. Unless they invite you in, church is all you get. I learned that "family" in the church means that I can pray for you when you need help or are going through something, but that doesn't mean that I will be there for you in other ways when something happens to you. I learned that when someone leaves the church, DO NOT CALL THEM. That was a hard one. Once a person leaves the church that you are attending, they do not want to keep in contact with you. So what you still have their phone number, physical, and email address. Delete it. Never call someone who left the church unless the call you first. I still have so many numbers like that in my phone and again, I learned this one the hard way....I am still learning this one. I learned that a lot of the leadership in black churches are all related. That was an interesting one to learn.

From churches in general, including non-predominantly black churches, I have learned all of the above plus more. From white churches, I have learned that racism doesn't exist so why talk about it. From white churches, I learned that black hair is so cute at church, but may not be professional. From white churches, I learned that black kids, though different from white kids, need to learn to fit into the "white society" or be medicated in order to do so. From white churches, I learned that it's okay to invite a few blacks, but too many blacks in their church makes them nervous. From white churches, I learned that majority of the music they sing will never be by black people...even if they do have a black token on the worship team. I have learned that white kids go on mission trips from a very young age and learn to be leaders in the church early in life, while black churches....not so much. I learned that white kids get scholarships, prizes, and awards inside the church....black kids, not so much. White kids go to Awana scouts and black kids, well the just have their own groups and clubs inside the church. I learned that it is better not to ask questions unless you are at an in-home bible study....and even then, from both churches, I learned that never ask questions about experiences that aren't "normal". Just sit there and listen and be quiet. When they ask you if you have any questions, they are just being courteous, but your response should always be no. I have also learned that if you are aligned with God like you say, then your words, behaviors, and reactions will be to. If they aren't, then you are being "fake" and not "real". This one was also a hard one to learn. Speaking in tongues is evident of the Holy Spirit and if you don't speak in tongues, then you don't have it. This one has been a weird one to know although I still don't get it.

So I went to this unnamed mega church and wanted to get the Holy Spirit. I have also been to a small local church and have tried to get the Holy Spirit. Now, I love my Father….there is no one who can tell me that I don't. For all the times in which I have tried to get the Holy Spirit, Bishops, Pastors, etc. have told me to go to the front, close my eyes, raise my hands, and say either "Holy Ghost" or "Thank you Jesus" repeatedly. I would continually do it, but then they come over to me and tell me to open my mouth and speak….and I am in my head like "speak what". I have tried repeatedly to do what I was told and every time, I feel like I am not good enough because maybe I just didn't do it right. Why does my Daddy give everyone else the Holy Spirit but not me. The last time I tried to get it, the prophetess told me to tell God that I wanted to live, but in the end I can't because I don't know how to live….I only know how to survive. I am done trying to get this Holy Spirit. It just makes me depressed every time I think about it. I love my Daddy so much but because other people say the actions speak louder than words, then apparently, I am not ready and am not trying hard enough to get it. I have even been told that I have to be sold out to God which I still don't know what that means yet either. All I know is that I love my Daddy with all of my heart. I love Jesus with all of my heart, and one day, I hope He thinks that I am good enough to be with Him. I just want my Daddy to hold me…nothing else. No mansions, no fancy garden, just my Daddy with me in His arms. Everything else, I don't understand, and maybe I never will.

The Power of Prayer

Prayer is a very powerful tool. There are many people out there who may not believe so, but I can only speak from my personal experiences. I talk to my Daddy quite a bit. It may not be the fancy way like missionaries and deacons, but I do talk to Him. I love my Father. I tell Him about my feelings and about how I try really hard to be a good girl, but how sometimes, I just can't get things right and I don't understand why or how. I don't really know how to pray over other people though. It is still confusing to me. Sometimes, when I don't know what to say to Jesus, I just recite the Lord's Prayer.

For me, prayer is a way to communicate with my Father. You can't just literally walk up to His door and knock, so you have to do it figuratively. I imagine that I literally walk up to His door, but I never knock. I barge right on in and say, "Daddy, I really need to talk to you". Life is full of surprises and this chapter will be full of what I think I can remember about my prayers, but maybe not what I actually remember. Answers to prayers can be positive or negative and positivity in my brain doesn't always stick.

So the very first answered prayer that comes to mind is my very first car…a 2003 Mitsubishi Endeavor LS…I still have it while I am writing this book. Hold up, let me back up a minute. It took me a very long time to even get my license. I had been told at nineteen by DMV that there was no one who could literally teach me how to drive because I was an adult. The only driving education classes that were out there were for teenagers. It wasn't until the age of twenty-seven that I found out about 911 Driving School. I got to learn how to drive by police officers. It was the coolest class I had ever been to and was a lot of fun. They taught me how to drive and I passed both my written and my behind the wheel test.

So, now we are up to speed. I needed a car. I had around $5500 and went into a used car lot. Now, I don't know how God speaks to everyone else, but for me, after I pray about something…a lot and sometimes, not enough, God gives me my answer. I walked into that car lot and knew nothing about cars. Jesus gave me the 2003 Mitsubishi Endeavor LS. I didn't test drive it, I just instantly fell in love with that one and that color…. navy blue. Little did I know that, that exact car would take me through some crazy obstacles. With that car, I packed up everything I could and I traveled across country from the East Coast to the West Coast during the winter with my 3-year-old daughter. I slid into a ditch in the median in some southeastern state along that route and had to pay $100 to get myself out with no scratches or anything wrong with the car. I stopped in a southern state and visited some people. The drive was amazing. Without all of these racist and hateful people, America is amazingly beautiful. Through Mount Swallowtail and the Novena Desert, I have seen some beautiful places. I have also traveled in that car from one side of the United States to the other and back. I have put a lot of miles on that car. The space is awesome and the seats for me are really comfortable. I have not found many cars with as big of a trunk as the Mitsubishi Endeavor LS. I shot my first full-fledged short film with that car. I had to pack the lights, the sound equipment, the apple boxes, the boom box and microphones, the camera and all of that equipment that goes with it, and everything else I needed for the film in that car. That car will always be my favorite. I have test driven a lot of cars through Enterprise and other car rental places, and still that Mitsubishi Endeavor LS will always be number one.

My next car was also a gift. After my Mitsubishi started having some issues, I really needed another car. I went to my Daddy and was gifted a used car no terms. My Honda Odyssey needed a little fixing up, but for the most part has also taken me through sometimes. At first, I was really upset about my Mitsubishi. I didn't see why God couldn't just fix His original gift to me, but eventually I grew to like the Honda. While not the same as my Mitsubishi and lacking a horn, I see value in all of God's gifts to me regardless of what they are.

There have been many other things that I have prayed for and have had answered. Being on Section 8, not having to panhandle again, not being homeless again, having a birthday party, graduating college, and many others were good prayers that were answered. When my cousin HL died before the age of 15 of brain tumors, that was a prayer that didn't go the way I wanted it to go. A Bishop said that many people asked for my cousin to be healed and in the end, he was, but just not in the way that everyone asked. HL had, had brain tumors since about the age of 5 and now he is gone. Not all prayers are answered or are happy, but in the end, Jesus still hears them.

I will always pray to my Father whether people believe in prayer or not. For me, prayer is not about getting them answered, but more about the action of talking to my Daddy. When God tells us to ask and states that we shall receive, it doesn't always mean that we will receive it how and when we want it. Because of the power of free will and sin, there will always be bad stuff happening to people until He comes back. It is true that the greatest thing that Satan ever did, was not try and create life himself, but was convincing the world he doesn't exist. For those who have never seen a demon, believe me....you don't want to. I am not scared of them, for I know who I am in Christ. For me, I feel protected in that God has covered me differently as an adult versus when I was a child. I may not always understand what, why, or how He does things, but for now, I am trusting in it. His love is everlasting and fulfilling. I can feel it. I see it, and I know it.

A Rose Among Thorns

First Lady has a very gentle touch. I love how her hugs make you feel better. She is very anointed, and you can feel it every time she opens her mouth. Her words are congenial, dove-like, merciful, and sweet-tempered. She tells you the truth, but in a way that is loving, compassionate, placid, empathetic, and serene. You know that she cares and has a really big heart. You can feel it, see it, hear it. She makes sure you know that she is imperfect and that if she ever does hurt your feelings, she doesn't mean to. Her ambience is enticing because her heart for God is so massive that you feel God's Presence in the church, her office, and her home even when she is not there. This presence quiets the soul, calms the spirit, and dries your tears. She is gracious as she is sweet. She makes you feel comfortable especially when you are feeling ugly and disgusting on the inside. She is truly the Proverbs 31 Woman and a Woman after God's own heart. I love my First Lady because she doesn't give up on me. She sees my heart. She sees how much I try, how much I strive for perfection. She is very humble and appreciative. She teaches me when I mess up. She doesn't belittle me or get irritated when I am myself and am sometimes immature.... she encourages me to be myself. Through our experiences, earthquakes, mistakes, hurricanes, blowups, and tornadoes can God truly mold us into who we are meant to be. She is my role model because of her character, her morals, her imperfections, and because of the love she continues to show other people. The mother of many, she would never turn away a broken child, she leads them to God in a way most people cannot. Thank you for loving and teaching me First Lady, Pastor, and Mother of the Church. You have no idea the impact that your love has had on me in my former years. You have no idea how much or how many you have healed just by your hugs and your smile. You have no idea the dark places you bring people out of with your kind and gentle words especially when they are considering some days to be their last. I pray that Satan will never be able to take those gifts away from you because the way you are, you save lives. Not by being a doctor or a psychologist, or even a lawyer, but by your love and by the love of Christ bursting from within you. God Bless You Saved, Sanctified, and Holy Ghost Filled, First Lady!

"A gentle answer deflects anger, but harsh words make tempers flare."

Proverbs 15:1 NLT

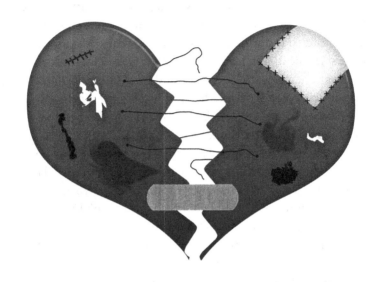

Being Baptized

All my life, men have been a symbol of pain and sex for me. I spoke to them either because I was sleeping with them or because they were sleeping with me. Being sexually abused and raped by many different men since the age of six, not knowing at what age my virginity was taken, and being trained by men to do what no child should have to do. By the age of nine, I had mastered the art of oral sex by my 22-year-old abuser. I became a ward of the state the month before I turned 13. Once I was in social services custody, the abuse never stopped there, and I was given the name, 'jailbait' by social services, which meant that I seduced grown men into sleeping with me and then afterwards I called it rape. They claimed that I was the reason for men wanting to sleep with me. At the age of 18, I was homeless, while still in social services custody. No one would help me and I didn't know the first thing about taking care of myself except by sexual means. So, a man offered me a roof in exchange for some time between my legs, and I agreed. I didn't know that I could get pregnant. I didn't know that I could get pregnant because all of the doctors that I had talked to stated that my insides were messed up due to all of the sexual abuse, but I got pregnant with a baby girl by a convicted sexual offender. As soon as social services found out that I was 3 months pregnant, they emancipated me, homeless and pregnant, I was alone. Around the age of 25, I was told by a Pastor that the reason why I had been sexually abused so much is because Satan had put a mark on my forehead that had to be removed. Around the age of 26, I was forced into prostitution by my own biological maternal parent. At the age of 32, I had my first boyfriend, which ended badly. To men, I was a Sexual Goddess, a Seductress, a Sex Queen that they had made. To social services, I was nothing more than a manipulator who men should watch out for and stay away from. I was the one who could take any man down sexually within seconds.

Who was I to Jesus?

When I came to the church that I am at, I had delivered a second child by means of rape in 2009 at the age of 27. I got to this church in 2014. I was not happy with men. I didn't want anything to do with them. The only way I wanted them touching me is if I said so. I had one body and I wanted to be in control. My motto was: It's my body and I say who can touch it and when. I got acquainted with the pastor's wife through a Super Bowl Party that my aunt had invited me to.

Now let's get another thing straight. I love Jesus, but I hated churches. I didn't want to see or hear of another church. My aunt had asked the pastor's wife to just talk to me at the party. Have you ever talked to someone and they made you feel instantly 'safe'? That was what it was like. First Lady opened her mouth and began speaking to me. Now I can't remember what she said, how she said it, or even what our whole conversation was about, but when she literally began talking to me, I forgot about my barriers and my walls and I just felt 'safe'.

After that party and I think one or two more Sundays at this church, I joined the church. I took their class 101, which was an introduction, but I slowly became attached to the Pastor's wife. She helped me to learn and grow, even though part of me was scared to let her in still. She taught me how to properly socialize....that was hard. Every time I would see her, I would run up and say hi and give her a big hug. I never spoke to her husband. I loved spending time with the Pastor's wife.

A year later at a harvest party, I ran up to give First Lady a hug and to say hi. She gave me a hug like usual, but this time her husband spoke up. I don't remember his exact words, but it was funny to me. He said something like, 'Do you see me standing here? You say hi, run up to her, and give her hugs and I don't get nothing. Can I get a little hello, Amen?' Again, I don't remember the exact words, but I remember that it was so funny to me. I just started laughing. From then on, I had started trying to say to hello to Bishop when I remembered. As time went on, there were these 'bread crumbs'. **Bread crumbs** are a series of connected pieces of information or evidence. There would be times when I really needed prayer and Bishop would be the only one there in the church that I knew I could trust. I didn't know anyone else and I didn't trust anyone else. I knew that Bishop knew First Lady and, in my mind, he's only safe because she is. Slowly, I began trusting Bishop. I got so excited when I got to the point that I was comfortable enough to ask him for hugs.

I took class 201 (a Christian class that focuses on Spiritual Maturity), and even started doing the Multimedia for this church, which allowed me to work for Bishop and First Lady. Even though I was their employee, I still always looked at and respected both First Lady and Bishop at this point as my parents, even though they weren't. I loved both of them.

Being a United States Orphan, left me pretty immature, naïve, young, and with a lot to learn. I was hurt, broken, lost, unloved, and lonely. It had always been just Jesus and I, but never people, Jesus, and I. There was healing going on every time I spoke with, talked to, hugged, and all the above the Bishop and Pastor's Wife. Other people looked at me and saw this grown woman disrespecting the Bishop and his wife, but the Bishop and his wife looked at me through God's eyes. There was healing going on for me. People told me that it was inappropriate to give Bishop hugs and that it was disrespectful for me to call the pastor's wife 'pastor' instead of 'First Lady'. I went and asked them about this, and they said that I was fine. I was allowed to give Bishop hugs and I was allowed to call First Lady 'pastor', but the beauty of it was.....First Lady explained to me why people were saying that it was disrespectful to call her 'pastor' instead of 'first lady'. I understood things with First Lady because she explained them, she broke them down for me so that I would know and grow. No one had ever done that before.

You know how funny God is? I was so upset with my youngest daughter one day. I was livid. I really needed First Lady. I only go to their house when I really need something. I realty try not to bother them at home. I was so mad. I went to First Lady's house and I was on the verge of crying, with my youngest daughter in hand. I just really needed First Lady to please pray and to help me....guess what? Only Bishop was home. OMG! I really needed First Lady, but again, I followed the bread crumbs and I told Bishop what was going on and how upset I was and everything. He said, "Breathe." LOL. It's funny now, but then not so much, but I understood. He talked to me and my baby girl cried next to the wall. Then he prayed, I felt better. My baby girl and I went home....bread crumbs. There were times when I really felt I needed to ask First Lady a question and she wouldn't show up for church. Yeah I had her number, but she might not respond as quickly as the question was burning my head and Bishop was right there...bread crumbs.

One Sunday, Pastor became a Bishop. By this time, I had also begun calling the pastor's wife, First Lady.

Sunday (6 Months Later) – Father's Day

Father's Day was always a hard day for me. I had a stepfather when I was little, but he didn't ever really claim me. I don't really remember him because my biological mom and he divorced when I was around 8 or 9. What's worse, my biological father died in 2013, but I didn't learn about it until 2015....2 months after I learned that my stepfather had passed away. I had been talking to my biological father on the phone and he was trying to get himself together so I could finally meet him in person, but death met him first. I will never know him. I am grateful that I did get the opportunity to find and communicate with him before his passing. Needless to say, that I don't like Father's Day. I actually despise it. I get panic attacks and

I hate being around a whole bunch of men on this day. I, however, ran the Multimedia at this church and Father's Day was important to some men. Saturday night, I called First Lady to tell her that I really didn't want to go to church the next day and why. She told me that we would do it together. We would pray that night and in the morning. We would conquer this mountain together. Surprisingly, after all that prayer, it really wasn't that hard. I focused a lot on doing my job and less on who was in the church building.

The Following Sunday – Day of Baptism

I went to church like normal. Bishop preached at both campuses. He had preached a similar message like he had before, but today something was different. His message was entitled, "Blessed Outside The Familiar". People had been asking me for the past few weeks if I was getting baptized, and I kept saying the same answer. I wasn't getting baptized. I had already been baptized plenty of times before. Why should I get baptized again? I had asked First Lady about baptism. I wanted to know more about the symbolism. She told me it was like a statement, a confession, of your love for Christ, like when a woman puts on her wedding ring to show that she is married. Still I said that I wasn't getting baptized again.

In Bishop's message, (Mark 8:22-26) he was talking about being blessed outside of your comfort zone.

> God is not found in our own comfort. Faith does not work in comfort. Anytime God calls you to do something, it makes you uncomfortable. God has to remove us from a place of comfort in order to get us to the new destination. You cannot grow in comfort. Some people will never grow because they never get stretched. They never get uncomfortable. Anytime you are trying to go to new places, anytime you are trying to achieve, you're going to be uncomfortable. You have to learn how to embrace it. Most of the time people fight it, instead of embracing it. You will only grow when you learn how to embrace your discomfort. I'm not comfortable, but I know that if God be for me, then who can be against me. ...and another thing, I can do all things through Christ, that strengthens me. How many blessings are waiting on you to leave your place of comfort.

After the second service, I asked Bishop some questions. See, I like to write, but I don't really like praying out loud. So Bishop said that after I write down my prayers, read them out loud. Every time you ask Bishop and First Lady a question, they aren't going to respond like 'man'. Because of the glory of the Holy Spirit, they respond the way that Jesus would have them respond. They communicate with you through the eyes, ears, and words of God. They aren't perfect, but everything they do, they line it up with the Bible, and they see people through God's eyes, not man's.

One of my jobs for this church is to edit the sermon, post it on the website, and upload it to the church software. I got stuck that day after I edited the sermon. I listened to Bishop's message about three times plus the time I had to edit it. His message this day touched my heart different from any other day. I am a runner. If things get too hard, I run. I don't run towards fire, I run away from it. I also was going to be taking pictures of the Baptism, so I was scheduled to be there anyway. However, today, I also followed the bread crumbs. Okay, Jesus, I went to my house and got a change of clothes and a towel, just in case. I still wasn't getting baptized. No problem. I kept telling Jesus....I am still not getting baptized. I wanted a CD to listen to in the car. I noticed a CD lying on the floor in a pile that was never even opened. I could hear the Holy Spirit tell me to pick it up. So I grabbed it. It was WOW Gospel 2002. I never even listened to it before this day. When I got to the church, I was asked again by a couple of people if I was getting baptized. I had to take pictures, so there was no way I would be able to get baptized, and besides, I had also learned that everyone was supposed to wear white. I had nothing white, not even at home. Not even less than 15 minutes later, one of the missionaries came back and told me that they had worked everything out, they would take the pictures in the beginning, and there were other missionaries wrapping ladies in white sheets in the back of the church. Okay, I get it, no more excuses. Jesus, I was getting baptized. It was different. For whatever reason, I felt different. I felt nervous. I felt uncomfortable....and to make matters worse, I had to go first.

As the missionaries in the back were preparing me to be baptized, I kept telling Jesus that I was tired of running. I told him that I was trying to surrender the best way that I knew how, but that I needed him to meet me half way because I didn't know what I was doing. I was walking on unfamiliar territory. I don't stay and fight, I run. I was so nervous. My mind kept racing, and I kept praying. Then service started and I saw them open the hatch to the water. It was in the floor. I had never seen a baptism in the floor before. That was different. I had always seen them behind the podium, choir, you know, kind of up high. Then they called my name. I walked to the water very nervous and quite afraid. I kept trying to remember that I could do this. Don't run! It's just water. I got in and it was cold. I could hear Bishop telling someone where to position their hands on my body so they could dunk me. I remember going down and coming up, but it was weird. I went down one way, and I remember when I came up, I felt different. I was still me, but just different. Also, Bishop was supposed to do the Baptism, but instead two of the deacons stepped in and decided to do it for him. It never even occurred to me that two men were touching me while I was being baptized until I was halfway through taking the baptism pictures. I realized that there were two men in the water. It wasn't that I thought they were females or anything else…I just never even noticed them. I knew they were there, but their gender to me was nonexistent. I didn't see them as male, female, or anything. I just didn't notice. It was weird.

This baptism was significant for me because I was growing. I was healing. I was moving. Bishop says that we aren't supposed to get stuck in the wilderness (Psalm 23:4), but that we are supposed to keep moving. For the longest time, I felt dead. I love Jesus, but I never understood why he has kept me a live all of these years. I have felt lost, but First Lady says that God has me right where He wants me. This baptism for me was special because I recognized the changed, the growth, the movement, the steps that God used to get me there. Every one of the steps listed above from 2014 until the Baptism is what I noticed that God used to prepare me for this Baptism. He blessed me with amazing leaders who have helped me to grow and learn. Leaders that don't judge me at every turn and obstacle that I face. They continue to teach me how to stand on my own two feet, so that someday, I may be a blessing for someone else. I have a new church, a new family, a new life, new people around me that love me, and it's not easy because every day I still struggle, but at least I know that I have help without the fear of being bullied, persecuted, 'stoned', or kicked out. I am loved and the Baptism for me was a new start to a new life that I am grateful to have the opportunity to live. I may not know yet why my Daddy (Jesus, God, and the Holy Spirit) has kept me alive, but someday, when the time is right, he will tell me. Until then, Bishop and First Lady are teaching me 'how to fish' so that I may one day feed my entire family and help someone else also learn 'how to fish'.

God Lifted Me Up

I was thinking
Of my life one morning
The things God has done
He saved my life
I could have been dead
But God abet me to live

Chorus:
God lifted me up
In time
'Cause he's not finished with me
I have a mission
That has to be done
Before I'm through
Yes God said he cares
For me
And he's not letting me go
I have a mission
That has to be done
God lifted me up

Deep in depression
Careless and hopeless
No love for me back then
Was my whole life

I didn't know what to do
But God showed me
How to live

Chorus

When help was needed
No friends could be found
No mother, father, or anyone else
I felt so alone
But God told me
'Bout his love

Chorus

Saved by his grace
And redeemed by his love
My father who died for me
On thee Calvary
No greater love
That I know of
And now I'm filled
With eternal peace

Chorus

You're Just Average

People say and write a lot of things about me. People look at me and wonder how I keep a smile on my face. How could I have gone through everything that I have gone through and still be so happy. Some people say that I make too many excuses. People have asked me how come what I have gone through doesn't really show on the outside. I am too fat. Some people have called me crazy. People have called me "jail bait" saying that I seduced grown men into sleeping with me and then called it rape when I was just 13. Some people have said that I shouldn't have kids because I will just do to my kids what my biological mother did to me. I am too immature and childish. Some people say that I make too many mistakes. People have called me average.

I say, I am not nor will I ever be just average. I am extraordinary. I am the Head and not the Tail. I am above and not beneath. I am the Light of the World because He who lives in Me is greater than he who is in the World. I am more than a conqueror. I am a child of the King. I am a chosen generation. I am a royal priesthood. I am a holy nation. I am Blessed. My Father loves me so much that He died for me. I am an astonishing work of art.

I am not nor will I ever be just average.
I am extraordinary!

Romans 8:31-39, John 1:12, Matthew 5:14-16, Ephesians 2:10, John 8:12, Deuteronomy 28:13, 1 John 4:4-6, 1 Peter 2:9, Galatians 3:26, 1 John 3:1, Psalm 47, Romans 8:2, Galatians 4:7, Ephesians 1:3, John 3:16, 1 Corinthians 6:19

My Place of Refuge

My place of refuge has no name. It is my special place that I can invite in anyone I want. There is no pain and suffering, crime and punishment, death and despair, or loss and abandonment. It is surrounded by a fourteen feet tall stonewall and has an area of about 700,000 square feet. Each horizontal row of stones is about one foot tall. The top horizontal row starts off having the color red. The rest of the horizontal row of stones follow suit in order of the colors of the rainbow; the second horizontal row being orange, the third being yellow, and so on and so on. The entrance to my special place has two pure golden doors. The doors have a total length of fifteen feet, and a total width of seven feet. Once inside the doors, you immediately notice a rainbow colored brick road. No buildings can be seen until you are one acre into my special place. In the very center of my special location sits the biggest apple tree that you ever did see. I would say that it is probably about three hundred feet tall, although I have never myself measured it. The tree has one acre of land all to itself surrounded by a river with a radius of seven feet and a depth of three feet. The tree's trunk though, does not cover the whole acre; only its branches do that. It produces such a huge variety of apples, not only a few kinds like the planet Earth knows of. You can talk to the tree, and it will give you an apple when you want one. The apples never fall off of the tree by themselves. Everything else in my special place encircles this acre that the tree stands on. It is kind of like a face on a clock. The apple tree sits in the middle, and my other landmarks are the "numbers" on the clock. The other landmarks that make up my special area include a labyrinth made out of rose bushes (that you can always find your way out of), a rose garden that grows with no thorns, my two-story house, a funhouse, a barn, a stable, a waterfall that flows into the river, and a vegetable garden that never runs out of veggies.

The Two-Story House

On the front of the house there is a huge picture of a rainbow. The rainbow starts at the bottom left corner of the house, just barely touches the top middle, and continues to the near bottom right corner. At the end of the rainbow sits a beautiful golden pot that has the word "heaven" repeatedly coming out of it and spilling on gorgeous green grass. Surrounding the rainbow you can see nothing but huge, fluffy, white clouds. Stained glass windows portraying portraits of me throughout my life (some including "the trinity"…God, Jesus, and the Holy Spirit) encircle about 80% of the house and are positioned in groups of four at each of the rooms. The roof is made up of two huge stained glass windows as well. One portrays a portrait of a beautiful white dove with three ribbons in its mouth, each representing a part of the trinity. The other shows a huge friendly looking lion surrounded by one type of every kind of animal that God has ever made. This house is made up of eight total rooms. My bedroom, my daughter's room, a grand and royal bathroom, and a guest room make up the upstairs rooms. The kitchen, the living room, another bathroom just as big as the upstairs one, and the dining room make up the downstairs.

The living room is the most significant spot out of the whole house. This room is where majority of my time is spent with the trinity and my daughter. It is about thirty feet square with the floor covered in soft, fluffy, multicolored carpet. It has a love seat, a couch that seats up to four people, and two recliners, that have been upholstered with multicolored rabbit furs distributed evenly around the room and have their backs pressed up against the wall. The loveseat and the two recliners each have a two feet tall round nightstand that accompany their right side. On each nightstand sits a clear vase of a range of colors of long-stemmed roses that never die. At the head of this living room sits a fireplace with a painted portrait of a rainbow colored three-leaf clover above it, each leaf containing one of the names of the trinity. On one of the walls there stands some stereo equipment in a wooden case with a glass door, and including two five foot speakers, one on each side of the wooden case. A ten-foot square compact disc stand is located on the right of the right speaker and holds a massive collection of a wide variety of Christian artists. A big flat screen television hangs on the wall, five feet from the ground, and about five feet from the fireplace …it only gets Christian channels. There is a three feet square, four-shelf bookcase underneath the television. A DVD/VCR combo sits on the top shelf, DVD/VHS tapes of assorted Christian cartoons on the second shelf, and the other two shelves consisting of DVD/VHS tapes of an assortment of Christian movies and on stage comedians.

My Place of Refuge Is The Safest Place In The World…

I Just Wish It Was Real

How Does The Use Of Myth, Story, and Fairy Tales Help As A Therapy For Abused Children

A bused children and young adults come in many different forms and fashions. They are everywhere and live in a variety of places and social economics, and also vary from age, gender, race, and sexual orientation. Some even live in foster homes, group homes, shelters, mental institutions, respite homes, and single or multifamily households, while others sleep on the streets. There many different forms of abuse, including verbal, sexual, emotional, physical, and spiritual; however abuse is still abuse.

According to Abuse In America and The National Child Abuse Statistics, *Children are suffering from a hidden epidemic of child abuse and neglect. One child abuse report is generated every 10 seconds, and over 3 million of them are generated each year in the United States alone; however, some reports have been known to contain multiple children. An estimate of about 6 million children were reported to have been abused and neglected in the year 2009 which was accumulated from over approximately 3.3 million child abuse reports. Child Abuse, alone, slaughters more than five children every day. Out of all the children that die from child abuse, approximately 80% of them are under the age of 4. Over 50% of child deaths that are caused from maltreatment are not even recorded at all, especially on death certificates. About 90% of all children under the age of 18 and/or 21 who are sexual abuse victims know their perpetrator in some way. 1 out of 3 women around the world has been beaten, coerced into sex or otherwise abused during her lifetime.* You may sit there in your chair and think, *I am not an abused person,* but the truth is *1 in 5 high school female students have reported being physically and/ or sexually abused by someone they had dated, and one in every three teenagers have been reported to have known a companion or associate who has been choked, hit, slapped, punched, or in some way physically, sexually, or emotionally hurt by their partner in some form or fashion. Girls who have been abused are also more probable to continue getting involved in other unsafe behaviors, and are also four to six more likely to get pregnant and eight to nine times more probable of having suicidal ideations and/or attempts. On top of all of this, children live what they learn and roughly 30% of all neglected and abused children will eventually end up abusing their own, allowing the cycle of abuse to continue. Of 21 year olds, 80% of them had reported being abused as children and met the criteria for at least one psychological disorder. Child abuse and neglect also costs the taxpayers money. In 2008, the annual cost for this abuse was $124 billion.*

Even more now than in all of our history, children do not grow up with the securities of a loving home, an extended family, or a well-integrated community. That is why fairy tales were invented. It is highly important to provide the children of today's present with strong and courageous heroes who have to go out into this big world all by themselves. Although some may find that behavior nescient and immature, these heroes find secure places in the world by chasing their accurate way with fathomless inner confidence. Children, today, like the heroes in the fairy tales, journey for a long period of time in isolation. Some heroes are helped by being in touch with primitive things, such as a tree, or an animal, or nature, and children are often more likely to feel in touch with these things as well, versus an adult. The destiny of these heroes convinces children that, even though they may feel isolated, alone, abandoned, scared, and like an outcast in this dark world, the path of his life will guide him slowly step by step and give him help where he needs it. Children require that reassurance that is given by the images of isolated people who are capable of attaining significant and rewarding connections with the world around them. Fairy tales are highly future oriented and lead children to comprehend in both the conscious and subconscious mind, in order to abandon their childish and immature reliant hopes and desires and reach a bigger satisfying self-sufficient entity and existence.

Fairy tales, myths, and stories can help as a therapy for abused children in many different ways. There are many different types of fairy tales that help children. Fairytales, also declared the "language of soul", are stories of fantasy adapted from folktales, myths, legends, and/or fables. Some, but not all, of these stories are blueprinted to amuse, entertain, enlighten, and inspire children. Folktales are fictional stories dealing with human relationships, morality, conflicts, human problems, and solutions. Myths are stories explaining the foundation of the world and is composed of cosmic issues, such as earth and sky, heaven and hell, gods and goddesses, and human beings. Myths are often regarded as authentic by affiliates of the group whose history is being described. Legends are stories relating incidents often thought to be valid, including tales of historical figures, heroic exploits, supernatural beings, and urban legends regarding presumed current events. Fables are stories in which animals elucidate human roles and delineate, exemplify, and depict moral teachings.

Preschool Express clarifies that fairy tales, myths, and stories help children learn educationally. With language arts children are introduced to and begin learning many new words and phrases. Children learn mathematics through the difference between sizes, opposites, contrasts, proportions, time, and order. Multi-cultural values are taught by children becoming aware of and learning to appreciate diverse cultures and types of people. Children will and love to act out fairy tales during play time thus learning drama and theaters thus learning drama and theater. Imagination Exploration is introduced where children will begin repeating fairy tales that they have read or heard to their friends. Sometimes they will even make up their own version of a fairy tale creating a whole new one altogether. Also fosters children to actually visualize every step of the story when reading or listening to it. Home Economics are introduced to children through various cooking projects and other house management skills.

Fairy tales, myths, and stories help children with emotional growth. For hundreds of years, fairy tales have illustrated people's lives, affirmed patterns of human behavior, centralized on human encounters, endeavors, contentions, complications, and resolutions, and recorded the long antiquity and ancient past of human conflicts. Fairy tales expose children to a variety of emotions, kinds of people, and a vast assortment of situations, seen also in their everyday life, in a simplistic and effortless to comprehend method. Children can watch and interpret how fairy tale characters have run into problems, situations, anxieties, faith and despair, confidence and low self-esteem, and then evaluate and apply this perception to real-life situations. Children can learn how to help others in difficult circumstances and also allow others to help them as well. Fairy tales can lower the phase of opposition and denial that a client, among depraved children and young adults have, and allow them more time to focus right on their abuse issues. Fairy tales can also grab them on such a fathomless emotional level, allow earnest, sincere, and grave discussions without close and personal disclosures, provide tender, non-menacing ways of examining challenging issues, objectify and universalize human conflicts, and assist children and young adults in figuring out their own thoughts and feelings. Fairy tales can equip, inspire, and embolden a victim to find deeper awareness, clearer self-understanding and creative ways to very arduous situations. They can also create their own ways or use the ones in fairy tales to solve their modern day problems.

Bettelheim states that fairy tales, myths, and stories help children learn the concept of good and bad morals. As a parent, we are continuously trying to shelter our children from all kinds of evil; however this can only be attained when awareness is created. Holding off the teaching of such facets to a stage when they are able to understand may be a little too late. Fairy tales, however, elucidate evil in a very delicate and fine tone, which not only creates cognizance, but also does not frighten them. Fairy tales transmit moral behavior to children and help them to establish, recognize, and use them correctly in their lives. Children learn to discern between good and bad. They teach them that good deeds lead to success and bad deeds get them nowhere. Polarizations, which rule and govern fairy tales, also control children's minds. People can either be good or bad but never in between. Chastisement (or the fear of it) in fairy tales and in life, is only an inadequate prevention to crime. Believing that crime doesn't pay is an even greater efficacious deterrent, which is why, in fairy tales, the bad person always fails to succeed. Goodness winning all the time is not what attracts the child's attention, but rather the fact that the child can simply relate to the hero throughout all of his long and hard journeys. Because the child can relate to the hero, he/she imagines that they are going through everything the hero is going through, thus suffering with the hero in trouble and celebrating when they are victorious. Children make this recognition all on their own and the internal and external conflicts of the hero imprint morality on them.

Works Cited

"Abuse In America." *The Hotline*. National Domestic Violence Hotline, 2004-2006. Web. 24 Apr. 2012. <http://www.thehotline.org/get-educated/abuse-in-america/>.

Bettelheim, Bruno. *The Uses of Enchantment: The Meaning and Importance of Fairy Tales*. New York: Knopf, 1976. Print.

Biechonski, Jure. "THE USE OF FAIRY TALES IN ADULT PSYCHOTHERAPY & HYPNOTHERAPY." *Iranpa*. Iranpa.org. Web. 12 Apr. 2012. <http://www.iranpa.org/pdf/034.pdf>.

ChildHelp. "National Child Abuse Statistics." *Prevention and Treatment of Child Abuse*. Sara O' Meara and Yvonne Fedderson, 1959-2012. Web. 24 Apr. 2012. <http://www.childhelp.org/pages/statistics/>.

Dieckmann, Hans. "Fairy-Tales In Psychotherapy." *Journal Of Analytical Psychology* 42.2 (1997): 253-268. *Psychology and Behavioral Sciences Collection*. EBSCO. Web. 12 Apr. 2012.

Hare, John Bruno, and Melissa Ellen Casey. "A STUDY OF FAIRY TALES." *A Study of Fairy Tales: Chapter I. The Worth of Fairy Tales*. Sacred-Texts, 2011. Web. 12 Apr. 2012. <http://www.sacred-texts.com/etc/sft/sft04.htm>.

Kiernan, MFT, Bette U. "The Uses of Fairy Tales in Psychotherapy." *Web. Mit.edu*. Web. 12 Apr. 2012. <http://web.mit.edu/comm-forum/mit4/papers/Kiernan.pdf>.

Padmaja. "Impact of Fairy Tales on Children." *Edurite's Official Blog*. Edurite Technologies/Manipal K-12 Technologies, 12 July 2011. Web. 12 Apr. 2012. <http://www.edurite.com/blog/impact-of-fairy-tales-on-children/1865/>.

Pardeck, John T. "Children's Literature And Child Abuse." *Child Welfare* 69.1 (1990): 83-88. *Academic Search Complete*. EBSCO. Web. 12 Apr. 2012.

Ucko, PhD, Lenora. "Why Folk Stories Are Valuable in Counseling." *StoriesWork*. StoriesWork. Web. 12 Apr. 2012. <http://storieswork.org/Instruction/whyare.htm>.

Walker, Steven. "Young People's Mental Health: The Spiritual Power Of Fairy Stories, Myths And Legends." *Mental Health, Religion & Culture* 13.1 (2010): 81-92. *Psychology and Behavioral Sciences Collection.* EBSCO. Web. 12 Apr. 2012.

Warren, Jean. "Learning with Fairy Tales." *Preschool Express by Jean Warren: Preschool Activities, Games, Songs, Crafts, Art, Music, Learning, Skills, Stories and Patterns.* Preschool Express. Web. 12 Apr. 2012. <http://www.preschoolexpress.com/learning-station11/learning-with-fairy-tales.shtml>.

Dealing With Rollercoasters

Life for me has been nothing but rollercoasters. Throughout my life, problems have seemed to constantly follow me. Being in constant pain for the past 18 years has been very depressing in itself. So much so that when my employment specialist started realizing how things were constantly happening to me, she told me jokingly that she thinks that there are minions all around me secretly making my life miserable and chaotic. My counselor told me that she thought that maybe I needed to smudge.

Smudging (and/or saging) is the common name given to the Sacred Smoke Bowl Blessing, a powerful cleansing technique from the Native American tradition. My ancestors have believed that all plants, animals, and nature is sacred and that sacred smoke uplift many vibrations and spirits and assist with magic. Smudging your sacred space, your home or office, or even your body with sage is like taking an energetic (and sometimes physical) shower, or doing a deep metaphysical cleansing. Smudging is the act of burning sacred herbs to transform and erase negative energy. The smoke from dried sage actually alters the ionic composition of the air, and can have a direct effect on reducing our stress response.

Despite everything that I have been through, I have made it by the grace of God to the age of 36. I also have a few coping skills that have also helped me to survive. I will not list all of them, but I will list the major ones. For starters, music has been immensely helpful to me. When I was in social services custody, I used to save my money just to buy CD's from the store. To this day, I have tons of CD's in my collection…even though I only listen to them when I am in a car that has a CD player. I was extremely happy when I finally got a Mac because now I could have all of my music on my iTunes account and play them on my iPod. I love creating a different playlist for every different situation, party, or event. It has been very helpful to me. I was mad however, when I learned that the only way to obtain music videos was to download them. I love music videos. I didn't understand why they didn't originally sell them like CD's.

From Disney's Descendants to Disney's Teen Beach, from Scotty McCreery to Florida Georgia Line, from Britt Nicole to Mandisa, from The Pointer Sisters to Darius Rucker, from Brooklyn Queen to Kenya Rock Star Madness Band, from Disney's Let It Shine to the Empire Soundtrack, from Michael Jackson to Diana Ross, from Ella Fitzgerald to Duke Ellington, Queen Latifah, Beyoncé, 2Pac, Nas, Queen McElrath, Esperanza Spalding, Insingizi, Chicago South Side Kids, R-Swift, Andy Mineo, Trip Lee, KB, Phyno, Ali Kiba, Alessia Cara, Kirk Franklin, Jagged Edge, Alvin and the Chipmunks, 3LW, Missy Elliott, Nia Sioux, Whitney Houston, Tye

Tribbett, Tyrese, Jojo Siwa, Will Smith, Logic, TLC, JLo, Ciara, Haschak Sisters, Khalid, KRS One, Taylor Swift, Mc Hammer, Brittany Spears, Yolanda Adams, Boyz II Men, Lady Gaga, Fifth Harmony, from R&B to Gospel, from Rap and Hip Hop to Country, from Pop to Jazz, from Blues, to Swing, and especially all things Disney, my iTunes has many songs that have helped me through a lot of tough times. There were times that I have wanted to die and then there were other times when I have felt loved. Then there were those times when I felt like everyone around me was fake and they were scandalous. I have felt those times when I was alone and especially those times when I was surrounded by people and felt lonely and super depressed. There are times when I have celebrated and event and other times when I filled my ears with celebrating music. Music is one of the most powerful tool and coping skill that I have. Without music, life right now would be so much harder. I have had to walk over 4 miles home with my daughter and music helped both of us get there. So I have an iPod and so does my daughter. She has all children's music on hers (no cursing or inappropriate music - I made sure of it) and I have a wide range of music on mine.

Church, despite its flaws, for me is one of the greatest coping skills. Hearing the word of God preached, encouragement from fellow church members, and fellowshipping with other saints is fulfilling. Bible studies at people's house, Super Bowl parties, birthday parties, weddings, Christmas, and Thanksgiving, church for me has become like my second family. It brings me great joy to feel the presence of God, even when you are not looking for it. It is a very overwhelming and warm feeling. Church is a place where I can feel safe, comfortable, and just be myself. Prayer rooms are great because you can go in there and prayer about whatever you need prayer over. When you go in the prayer room, there is comfort knowing that, that room was already prayed over and anointed before you went in there. A war room is a type of prayer room that you have in your own place of residency. It is a place to conduct spiritual warfare. It is more powerful than just going to church because, now instead of church maybe like one to four times per week, you can go into your war room, pray, worship, anoint yourself, and everything else that you need to do in there. If you have never felt the presence of the Holy Spirit of Jesus, then hopefully someday you will. There are songs that talk about how powerful Jesus' name is but until it is put into action, that's when you actually see things happen.

Exercise is another great coping skill. I, however, cannot really exercise without music. There are times when I would need to get out and get some fresh air, so I would walk 4 miles with my daughter with our iPods on. The hard part is when I am not able to do that because of my child. My daughter can only do so much and I can't leave her at home by herself, so it becomes difficult. Walking is very helpful for me and has been an amazing tool, except when it is raining....and it rains here a lot.

Right now, there is a distinct possibility that I may have people who care about me. People who, in the event of an emergency, will drop everything to either help me or to find someone who can. Just because I have people who care about me, doesn't mean that I am not lonely. I don't have friends that I can talk to when I need to or hang out with me once a month. Loneliness is like darkness, empty and void and heavy. When I want to go somewhere, I have learned to go by myself....fill my emptiness with things and outings with myself. My next coping skill that I use is emotional spending. Before I use this coping skill, I always make sure that my basic bills (rent, electricity, water, and gas) are paid for. I have been homeless before and will fight to make sure that doesn't happen again. I panhandle for rent when I don't have enough money or work to even have anything...including a bar of soap. Emotional spending isn't always spending money on things that I don't necessarily need because I never do that. I take myself to iHop, Hometown Buffet, or other restaurants when I am feeling down. Sometimes, it just means going for a walk by myself in a wooded area and listening to my iPod Shuffle. I like walking on the beach (without kids or other child/adult complainers), hiking (without kids or other child/adult complainers), camping (without kids or other child/adult complainers), going out to eat (without kids or other child/adult complainers), or to an amusement park (without kids or other child/adult complainers). I look around the house for things that could make my life easier, like a juicer, or a rice cooker, or a veggie steamer. Oh man, there are so many kitchen appliances these days that really come in handy and make cooking and baking so much easier. My daughter needs clothes desperately and I go shopping for her. Cleaning supplies are needed around the house so I go shopping for them. If you really look around your house and upgrade everything in it, you will find that you spent more money upgrading everything than you will just shopping for unnecessary items. A new computer desk, a new couch, a new entertainment system.....oh and don't even let me get started on the Walmart and IKEA stores. If you have an emotional spending problem and you have a lot of money....stay far away from Walmart and IKEA. There are so many gadgets that are "As Seen On TV" in those stores that are supposed to make your life easier....

For instance that pineapple cutter/corer. Now I really love pineapples, but this gadget is amazing. I bought this one day and in less than 10 minutes, I had eaten a whole pineapple. Yeah emotional spending for me is so bad. I used to be obsessed with CD's and then the Mac and iPod came out. Then I was obsessed with DVD's and board games (still am). I have a whole collection of DVD's which is great because I have a child who likes watching children movies. I have different sections: the black movies, the Tyler Perry Movies, Christian movies, Disney Princesses, Disney movies, Thriller, Sci-Fi, Horror, Adult Drama, Teen Drama, Children's TV Shows, Children's Comedy, Adult TV Shows, and Adult Comedy. If you have never seen Mrs. Cantaloupe, I strongly encourage you to watch it.....hilarious.... Black Gospel Comedy.

Video Games are next, of course. The idea of being someone else other than yourself is a great stress release, but is also very addicting. When you feel like you hate your own life and don't want to be in it anymore, a video game can be a way to get away from your life for a while. I used to be addicted to Sims. That is one of the worst games for this type of situation. With customizable characters, extension packs, and real-life circumstances, Sims has changed a lot since about 2003 when I think is when I first started playing it. It will be even worse when Sims goes VR. I recently started playing a game called Choices and that's a really fun game, but costs too much for my bank account. I also love farm games like Township, Gardenscapes, and Farmville. I can't build my own farm right now or even grow my own food, so I do it virtually. Other games I like include Civilization, Hasbro online board games, Game of War, Forge of Empire, Merge Dragons, Candy Crush, and Dance Central. Now I use apps like AppLike, Fitplay, and Mistplay to play games for cool gift cards and even money.

The very last coping skill that I use is kind of abnormal, I guess. Masturbation is supposed to release endorphins that make you feel better and relieve stress. The hormone prolactin also helps you to fall asleep when you are all done. I realize that there are a lot of people who think that masturbation is wrong and disgusting. I know that because they have told me. A first lady of a church once told me that there is no biblical basis for masturbation being a sin, but it does compete with a person's mate. Since I do not have a mate and no one will probably ever be interested in me (because of how many times I have been raped), then I am good. Masturbation is also great exercise as well. My legs always feel like I have had a huge work out afterwards. Masturbation has helped me during some really hard times especially when I am lacking self-confidence and unattractive. The hard part comes in when I want to be touched by another human being and there is no one around but me, but hey since men don't really care about me, maybe I will get one of those male robots when society advances their technology and what they can actually do.

Nobody's Perfect

In a perfect world, nobody has any flaws. There is no hunger, fits of rage, sexual immorality, pain, orgies, greed, jealousy, impurity, factions, dissensions, witchcraft, hatred, discord, selfish ambition, debauchery, envy, idolatry, drunkenness. There is only peace, love and harmony. In a perfect world, no one would go without and everyone would probably be very similar. In a perfect world, there would no natural disasters, wars upon wars, or murder. In a perfect world, there would be no money because there would be no need for it. In a perfect world, looks wouldn't even matter, but we are human, living in a very imperfect world.

I have learned over the years, that people are imperfect. They will fail you every time. A first lady once told me that even on her best day, she will still fail me and let me down because she is human. People change like the wind. Some may be more consistent than others, but even with time, they change, even if just a little. Everyone has flaws, no matter who it is…well, unless it's a robot. However, even a robot has some sort of flaws because an imperfect person built it.

A first lady also once told me that feelings are fickle. One day you feel like chocolate and the next you don't. Our feeling about each other are like children. One minute they be mean to each other, the next minute they are best friends. Sure there are those people who hold grudges, but holding grudges usually only harms the person holding them. The word is full of a vast amount of different personalities, attitudes, and behaviors. We are never going to get along with everyone.

Sometimes, when I feel like people don't care about me, I have to take a step back and try to observe my life as I would a television show. I have to see the bigger picture and really focus on the positives, instead of the negatives. Sometimes, people have their own reasons for treating certain people certain ways. Sure there are those people who are just mean, but even then they still have reasons for doing what they are doing. I have found that sometimes the reasons don't even involve me and sometimes they do.

I am not perfect either. I have many flaws. There have been people that I have hurt over the years as well, maybe not intentional, but I still hurt them. Just because I may not be able to remember all of the things that I have done, doesn't wash or wipe away what I have done. Someone may write a book about me someday, but the point is, that we are all imperfect in a very imperfect world. It doesn't make it any less depressing knowing that though because we are human beings with feelings.

Forgiveness is a powerful thing. Forgiveness is the act of stopping your own anger and resentment against someone else for something they did to you. The reason why it is important to forgive is because we should always remember that someone in the world has already forgiven us. In Matthew 18:21-35, the bible talks about a man who had an enormous amount of debts. The man went to the king and pleaded with him and begged him for mercy. Then the king had compassion on the man and canceled his dept. However, when another person owed the man some money, not even as much as the man had owed the king, then the man got angry, resentful, and physically violent toward that persona and refused to forgive that person. The King stepped in and convicted the man, threw him in jail, and made him pay back everything he had originally owed the king.

Forgiveness is very powerful, but sometimes, I am not able to remember a lot of good things that happen in my life. There used to be a saying that simply said *that's a kodak moment*. What that meant was that the scene being played out was so beautiful that it needed to be captured on film. A picture is worth a thousand words. Capturing those moments, taking notes about them, and adding them to a photo album will sometimes help me remember the 'good' times.

For my 36th birthday, I had never felt so loved in all of my life. My biological mother fixed one of my cars so that I could drive it. She also cooked and threw me a party. I haven't had a birthday party like that since I was about 11 years old. A lot of people who loved me really showed up. Despite the gifts that everyone gave me, what touched me most was that they came to my party and I got to fellowship and spend time with them. I was even face timed by people who couldn't show up. One person sent me this really cute little teddy bear video on my phone that sung happy birthday to me in their voice. I also got a special card from an uncle who I hadn't talked to in a very long time. I took a group picture that day so that way I could always remember what a wonderful birthday party that was. Time to me is more precious than money. What I realized was that at the end of the day, people really do care about me. I just have to take a moment, step back, and remember the good times. I will never forget how special that birthday year was. That same year, six months earlier was when I had graduated from college. First lady gave me these beautiful roses. They were so breathtaking and smell up my whole apartment. A lot of people showed up to my graduation. I got quite a bit of gifts including the heavy candy and gum necklace, and jewelry, flowers, balloons, and more. Afterwards I was invited to an African party with some of my friends from this African celebration that I belong to. They were hosting it for graduates.

Not only did we have that one that night, but about a month later, we had another one.

I remember one early morning, I had my biological maternal parent's car. I had so much on my mind that I locked the keys in her car accidently. I didn't have the money to get the door open. I called First Lady to see if she could take me from one city to another to get the extra key from my biological mother who was at work. First Lady worked in The Pacific Northwest, so I thought that if I could catch her, then I would be fine. She wasn't planning on getting dressed that early and I interrupted her day with a problem that I had. However, she came and picked me up and took me to a different city than I was in to get my biological maternal parent's key and then drove off to work even though she didn't have to.

There was another time when I had tried so hard to pick up my daughter from a Christian summer camp by the time they closed. Both of my cars at the time weren't working so I had to take the bus. In a car, it would have taken me 15 to 20 minutes max. On the bus and in traffic, it took me 2 hours. By the time, I got there, I didn't have enough bus money for my daughter to ride, so I said to myself that we would walk from one city to another, over an interstate bridge. I picked up my child and we began walking. After about 2 to 3 minutes, the missionary from that church drove by and told us to get in the car. She stated that she would drive us home.

There are a lot of stories that are blessings in my life, but taking the time to remember them or capture them on film, it reinforces the thinking and mindset of the fact that people really do care and love me. I know that if there was ever anything that would ever happen to me, the people who cared about me would be sad. If I was to ever get raped or beaten or robbed or anything, I have people who really care about me. It is comforting to know that. We do need each other. Humans need connection, love, support, and forgiveness to survive. Seeing goodness and love through the shame, past pain, depression, and brokenness is like trying to see in a smoky burning building. It doesn't mean it's not there, it just means you have to try harder to see it. Goodness, love, and mercy can actually be closer than you think. However, if you give in to the loud, boisterous, and vast darkness and never try to see it, then you will always stay in the darkness…unless there is something or someone positive and good that you will allow to help pull you out. It's not easy and it takes hard work every second, minute, hour, and day. The more you train your brain to look at and remember positive things, the more your brain will get accustomed to seeing them.

I am still working on this. It is very difficult. A lot of times I fail.... actually, most times I fail at this, but I never give up. I keep trying. Even when I want to give up, I have people who refuse to give up on me, who call me, and post things on Facebook in order to get my attention (like Lẹwa Ubunifu, where are you). I love them for taking the time to get to know me and for loving on me. I honestly can't remember every circumstance that people have showed me that they love me or care about me, but I can certainly try to remember as many as I can. I am now trying to setup my own boundaries and love people where they are. I don't know much about forgiveness or even how to do it, but I have to start with me. When someone or something doesn't respect my boundaries, I cut it off at the source. I can't expect everyone to love me, but I can set standards of what I do and do not want. I try not to hate anyone, but just be "done" with them. In the end, I also try to forget the negatives, even when I am very unsuccessful at it. I also try to not judge other people unless they step into my personal space, even though I sometimes step into theirs. I am learning that my life is what it is and that I have to love people where there are, even if they are not close to me. I keep people at a distance so I never get hurt. People will always make mistakes. I am learning to keep myself protected because after all, Nobody's Perfect.

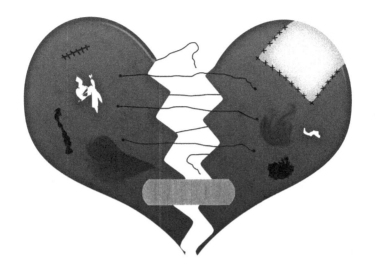

ABOUT THE AUTHOR

Entrepreneur. Single Mother. Author. Multimedia Specialist. Lęwa Ubunifu is a multi-talented and creative human being that was gifted and blessed with "creativity". Through life, business, and her personal life, she is full of artistic surprises. Through animations, graphic designs, cinematography, web page development, photography, and many other fashions of multimedia, her work continues to inspire others.

Printed in the United States
By Bookmasters